AF589474

A Star Is Porn

A Star Is Porn

BREAKING BARRIERS AND BARING IT ALL

Domonique Simone

Copyright © Deirdre Morrow

First print June 2023

CONTENTS

FOREWORD

Sex was everywhere, and I was right there in the middle of it. Half-naked photos of me were plastered in the windows of video stores throughout Times Square. My name – Domonique Simone – flashed in bright lights on the marquee at Show World, better known as the Emporium of Flesh.

The streets were full of hookers in G-strings and fur coats. Beautifully made-up transsexuals teetered on glittery stilettos, playing peekaboo with their dicks swinging. The air reeked of urine as homeless people ducked in and out of alleys to buy drugs. Transients and addicts curled up in doorways under the flicker of neon strobes.

Every other store was a porn or sex shop. Prostitutes in micro-mini skirts and gogo boots openly approached men in cars. Even the police horses had hard-ons as they clopped by, attempting to maintain a semblance of order.

Times Square back then was like the Las Vegas of sex, buzzing with a raw and dark energy of carnal pleasures. This was the early 1990s, pre-Mayor Rudy Giuliani, who would later come in and clean up the city.

I was 22 and already one of the most famous female African American adult film stars. It was crazy seeing my name in lights. Up until now, I'd been making adult films in my insulated world in Los Angeles. The adult film community was tight, and we were like family. But deep down I am very shy. Without an audience, it was easy not to think about the films being released in the world and who might be watching them.

In New York, it felt raw to have men whistling at me and calling my name like they knew me as I walked by. This was the first time I was able to see it with my own eyes: the darkness that fills the world, intensified by raw passion and sex.

The night I made my debut at Show World, where I would dance three shows a night and autograph Polaroids with fans for $50 a pop, it was like entering a circus. A guy with a bullhorn acted as ringleader, shouting out his wares to attract customers: "We've got girls, we've got boys, we've got trannies." There were four floors of debauchery in the Flesh Emporium, referred to by many as the "McDonald's of sex."

I ducked under the muscular arm of my bodyguard as he led me through the throngs of men gathered outside the front doors. We walked past the first-floor peepshows, where customers deposited coins to watch women take off their clothes. A curtain opened to a woman behind glass in various stages of undress; the more money inserted, the more clothes came off. Someone told me a girl had been killed in one of those booths, and the haunting feeling of that death hung over me as I climbed up to the third floor to take the stage.

I did my best to avoid seeing the faces in the crowd. The dimly lit auditorium was packed full of men from all walks of life: from the Wall Street executives in their three-piece suits to derelicts hustling for change on street corners.

Only an armed bodyguard stood between me and these hundreds of men, all of whom were undressing me with their eyes, not long before I would do it myself. I didn't want to know their thoughts about what they wanted to do to me; I didn't think I could handle it.

I'd never been a good dancer, but I acted the part, blinking under false eyelashes and heavy make-up as I gyrated under the hot lights and slowly slipped my clothes off. I had an arsenal of costumes that I tried out each night. Sometimes I'd be a cowgirl; others I might be an Egyptian goddess or a virginal bride in a white, lacy wedding dress.

I tried hard not to lock eyes with the men as they pulled out their dicks or masturbated with hands in their pants while sitting in those cum-stained, red velvet theater chairs. Sometimes, they'd be sitting right next to each other as if jerking off in a public space was an everyday, natural thing. I never got used to the raw sight and sound of a man's desperation when he came, hearing the guttural animal noises. (To be fair, those noises don't even come close to the man who panted like a dog when he came.)

Between sets, I downed shots and got high to make

myself get back up there onstage and do it again. At the end of the night, I donned a pair of sweats, a baggy sweatshirt, and a pair of oversized sunglasses and shot up to the fourth floor where I watched the hermaphrodites and transsexuals put on a show of their own.

Like a thief in the night, I hid out in the back row, just watching. The transsexuals swung their penises in guys' faces, the reverse of what was happening to me downstairs. I found it oddly satisfying, seeing the men have it shoved back in their faces, literally. Up on the fourth floor, there was no holding back. Men would sit on chairs in the center stage, jacking off as the audience went wild for the depravity.

Looking back at my younger self, the experience was actually pretty horrifying. It didn't seem that way at the time, though. I was at a point in my life where people wanted to be around me, but I couldn't differentiate if it was because I was a famous porn star or if they truly wanted to be my friend. Whom did they care more about: Dominique or Deirdre?

Sometimes I felt like a ragdoll, just there for men's pleasures, whether we were filming a scene together or they were watching my films in the comfort of their own homes. It was hard to ascertain my truths, to balance the work I did as Dominique while staying true to Deirdre, who I really was (and really am).

I often felt like I had lost my sense of humanity and was being plunged into this debauched, swirling tunnel of dark pleasures, where sex is traded as a commodity, drugs and alcohol flow freely, and you're washed up and retired by the time you're 30.

This was a world many people deemed evil because they were so shocked that someone could commit sexual acts on film for a living. It's what I call dancing with the devil.

I once read a quote that money changes people; if we don't remain vigilant and ask questions, we will go the way of other institutions. Pornography is intended to simulate eroticism rather than aesthetics or emotions. In other words, it's an industry focused on making money, not doing any greater good than fulfilling sexual fantasies, no matter how depraved.

What was the cost of engaging in risky, reckless, or potentially immoral behavior? That would be for me to find out.

How exactly did I get so far from home, from a small town in Georgia? On one hand, I was one of the most famous African American female adult film stars in the world with 300 films under my belt by the time I retired at age 27. On the other, I was still a girl from Georgia, who'd grown up loved and protected by my grandma.

Somewhere along the way, my life had taken a wild turn.

A STAR IS PORN
Breaking Barriers
and baring it all
DOMONIQUE SIMONE

1

DOWN-HOME GEORGIA GIRL

My birth was a surprise to everyone, including my mother. While the rest of her high school class in Valdosta, Georgia were tossing their caps in the air and collecting their diplomas, she was giving birth to me in a hallway in a local hospital outside of the emergency room. She was 16 years old when I was born on June 18th, 1971.

She didn't even make it into the emergency room. It was that close. She hadn't told anyone she was pregnant – including herself. Nine months of denial and praying that there was no baby growing inside of her did not have the outcome she was hoping for.

Nobody, however, was more surprised than my grandmother, a strict Southern Baptist woman who lived and died by the Bible.

It was news to her that her teenage daughter was pregnant, let alone actually having a child. Up until the moment of my arrival into the world, she thought my mother was just getting chubby from her after-school job at Shoney's, a drive-up fast-food joint where she delivered trays of hamburgers and fries on roller skates. She managed to do that even while she was pregnant.

Not long before going into labor, my mother complained of a stomachache. My grandmother, a typical Southern woman, gave her some castor oil to relieve the pain. It didn't work. Finally, my grandmother drove her to a nearby hospital and was shocked to see the crowning of my head as the doctors rushed to her aid.

"Are you pregnant?" my grandmother asked incredulously minutes before I was born.

Yes, she was pregnant.

As much as my mother had pretended she wasn't for the last nine months, I was quickly making my entrance into the world.

My mother somehow had managed to convince herself she wasn't pregnant. When her stomach started to push out, she tried to hide it under baggy clothing, telling herself that it was the Shoney's food, not a baby, making her gain weight. Not even her younger sister knew that she'd had sex, much less that she was pregnant. She didn't take a pregnancy test or go to the doctor. She definitely knew nothing about prenatal vitamins, let alone diapers or formula.

It must have been a really scary thing for her, being a religious, teenage, Black mother in the South. It's not surprising that she somehow managed to psychologically block it out.

So she didn't tell anyone. She didn't even admit it to herself, hoping that this was all just a bad dream she would soon wake up from.

My father never knew about me. He was a little bit older than my mother, and they met when they were both in high school. At 18, he enlisted in the Army, but he wasn't in the service long before he got into a fatal car accident. He broke his neck and died before my mother had a chance to tell him she was pregnant.

The doctors kept me in the hospital for a few days, since I'd basically been born on a gurney in a hospital hallway. After we left the hospital, I went home to live with my grandmother in a two-story brick townhouse in a housing project in Valdosta, Georgia.

Once my mother came home, my grandmother moved my bassinet into her bedroom. My mother might have put up a bit of a fuss, but I became her baby. My grandmother held no more anger at my mother for lying and hiding her pregnancy for so long, only love for her first granddaughter, who would also act as her youngest child.

My mother lived with us for a while but then moved in with a friend in town. It was here she met my future stepfather, who was visiting from West Virginia. He asked my mom to move there with him, and she saw that as a chance to go to college and have a better life than she could on her own.

I don't blame her. A Black, teenage, single mother in Valdosta didn't stand a chance. There weren't many opportunities for a woman with no education back then, especially a Black woman, and my mother wanted to make something of her life.

Apart from a winning football team – the Valdosta Wildcats – the southern city of just over 50,000 people didn't have a lot to offer. So my mother finished high school that summer and left for a better life. It was a hard decision, but she did what was best for both of us. I knew this, but it didn't make it any easier, at least in my young mind and heart.

She and my stepfather would come back to visit me and my grandmother twice a year. These were some of the best – and worst – memories of my childhood.

My mom would usually visit for the Fourth of July and around Christmas. I remember eagerly waiting at the screen door when I knew she was coming, agonizing over every moment until they would pull into the driveway. Sometimes, she would call ahead and say they were a few hours out, and I would sit in front of the door, peering through the mesh as I waited to see their car. When they pulled into the driveway, I shot out of the door to greet her.

This feeling was gut-wrenching; the anxiety of waiting to see the person I loved the most. It's a memory I vividly remember, and flashing forward years later, one I would have to relive when separated from my children. History has a funny way of repeating itself.

I remember all of the excitement surrounding those visits. It was so much fun having my mother around. She would take me into town to go shopping, and the two of us would come home with matching outfits. My grandmother didn't have a car, so these trips were the rare times I actually got to go to the mall.

My cousins and other family members would also come over, and it would be this weeklong celebration. We'd cook and make cakes, sing and dance, and it felt like being a part of a big family.

I would be sad on the first day, knowing my mother would soon be leaving. Eventually, I would put those feelings to the side, only to be emotionally destroyed at the end of the week when it was time to say goodbye. Another six months of waiting. That was the toughest part about those visits: knowing that they would come to an end and I would be back to waiting for her to pull into the driveway once again.

The pain of these goodbyes hit me in the pit of my stomach. I would try to put it off for as long as I could, clinging to my mother's legs and bawling like a baby, silently praying that she would change her mind and tell my stepfather that they were staying in Georgia. She'd cry too, most of the 13 hours it took to get home, she later told me.

I carry that pain with me even to this day. Later in life, after undergoing therapy, I learned the term "separation anxiety." That's what I went through as a child. I still don't like to say goodbye to people and I have an inherent fear of being left behind.

My grandmother did her best to distract me, but I would

typically cry through the night and the entire next day. I'd go to my room and be comforted by the Michael Jackson posters Scotch-taped to my walls. I felt so alone.

It wasn't that I didn't like living with my grandmother. I did. She took great care of me, and I knew if I had gotten into that car with my mother, I'd likely have cried and asked her to turn back around. But there is just something about the mother-child bond that I was missing out on, seeing my mother only twice a year, and it was difficult to deal with. An issue like that leaves a permanent fissure.

But ultimately, I had a good life with my grandmother, whom I loved more than anyone else in the world.

Looking good was important to my grandmother. In her prime, she had been a young, beautiful woman who worked for Ford in Detroit, making a lot of money. But when she had her first child out of wedlock, she was forced to quit her high-paying job and go on welfare. From there it was straight to the housing projects where she became a beautician. She made her living helping people look good.

My grandmother was tough, but she also doted on me. She made sure that my hair was fixed up every day and dressed me like a little doll. She washed my hair every weekend and pressed it with a hot comb. She wanted a better life for herself and us, something outside of the projects. She'd lost her dream by getting pregnant, and that stuck with her. As a young girl, I sensed my grandmother's depression. Sometimes she'd sit in her chair at night, staring into the distance as if lost in another lifetime where anything was still possible and all she had to do was reach.

I think my mother's pregnancy hit my grandmother hard. She saw history repeating itself: another young, Black woman getting pregnant out of wedlock. Another mouth to feed.

A year after my birth, when my aunt, my mom's younger sister, announced she was pregnant, my grandmother had a fit. She kicked her out before the baby was even born. I think my grandmother resented that her younger daughter could be so stupid. Hadn't she learned anything from her sister's mistake? Or hers? My grandmother couldn't get over it and had no patience for such idiocy, watching someone repeat the same history that she'd closely watched.

My aunt always seemed to resent me after that. I think she thought I was "saved" by my grandmother, while her own child had been tossed out on the street.

Given her daughters' mistakes and her fear of God, my grandmother was really strict with me. From an early age, I wasn't allowed to run wild like the rest of the kids. Instead, I had to sit on the front porch where she could see me. The other neighborhood kids could visit and play jacks and sit and watch all the people go by.

The projects – or PJs as they were called – were my home. In some ways, it wasn't so bad. It was nice that no one really cared about how much money you had. Everyone was like a family. Neighbors would ask other neighbors to watch their kids while they went to work. They'd keep an eye out to make sure that people weren't going in and out of their homes, including ours. We knew not to let strangers in the house or we'd get our asses whipped. It's not like that these days, when you have to beware of your neighbors. Back then, we had a strong community among the families in the projects.

Every once in a while, my grandmother would let me walk to the store with my friend Cedric Hollis, whom we called Sa Sa. He was the only person my grandmother really trusted. All the girls in the neighborhood loved him. He taught us how to dance and helped us put our outfits together. I recently learned that Sa Sa passed away. I was devastated by this because he was part of the sweeter side of my childhood.

Besides Sa Sa, my grandmother made it very clear that I wasn't to mess around with boys, and to keep me out of trouble, she sat me down with her in front of the television to watch daytime soap operas. Her favorite was *The Young and Restless*, and I can't count how many hours I sat there glued to the television, watching shows with her. She would give me my times tables to practice, so I memorized numbers during the commercials. But all that drama from the soap operas definitely left a mark on me, and as an adult, I got pretty good at mimicking it.

Despite her regrets, my grandmother made the best of her life. She kept our apartment as neat as a pin. No dishes sat on the counter for more than a few minutes and our furniture was wrapped in plastic. My mom tells me stories about my grandmother waking them up in the middle of the night if there was one dish in the sink. To this day, I do not go to bed without a clean kitchen.

Along with being strict, my grandmother was also incredibly religious and overprotective. As a child, she wouldn't let me go anywhere by myself and made it clear that boys were evil. I got whooped a lot for acting up: she'd make me go out into the yard and pick my own switch (tree limb) to get spanked with. Even though I would always pick the smallest or thinnest switch, it did not make a whole lot of a difference. It was still painful as hell.

Once, I was playing hide-and-go-seek and got my hair caught in the springs while hiding under my bed. For whatever reason, this made my grandmother really angry and she started whipping me. I tried to get away but tripped and hit my head on the end table and my forehead started bleeding. It scared us both, but she didn't take me to the hospital, and it didn't even dawn on me to call the police. The police would have just laughed at me and told my grandmother to beat my ass for wasting their time. That's just the way it was back then: you never turned to the police unless someone was shooting at you.

I knew my grandmother loved me, but sometimes, her temper scared me. I promised myself that when I grew up and had kids, I wouldn't lay a hand on them.

Apart from my grandmother, there was my uncle, who was eight years older than I was and more like a brother than an uncle. He teased me like a brother and enjoyed tormenting and scaring the shit out of me. I was terrified of horror films, and he liked to scare me just to get a laugh. After watching *It's Alive*, a low-budget horror movie about killer babies, my uncle told me that the babies were real and were coming after me to kill me in my bed after I went to sleep. I think this teasing is the reason why I can't handle sleeping in the dark to this very day.

My uncle could also be pretty cruel. I was a terrible tattletale, and he would retaliate even more when I got him in trouble. One day, he was angry because I tattled on him for having someone in the house when my grandmother wasn't there, so he tied me to my bed, stuck straight pins into my bottom, and had my cousins yell "stick her, stick her" to make them laugh.

The teasing was all in fun, and the two of us were thick as thieves. He was also very generous with me. I remember being a little girl and watching him cry at Christmas because I was the youngest and would get a lot of gifts. He had to go without. This makes me very sad to this day.

As a kid, I didn't realize there was anything different about him. I didn't find it weird that he dressed up like a woman and went out with men. I just knew he was my uncle and I loved him. He was an old-school drag queen and went out at night to do shows. In my mind, he was like a magician. I still remember watching him get ready and the way he danced around the room. He taught me everything I know about clothes and makeup, and he taught me how to dance. He even made me Wonder Woman bracelet-cuffs in his shop class and showed me how to master the Wonder Woman diva spin. I always think of him when I see Wonder Woman.

I thought he was glamorous and I loved watching him put on his makeup and his fancy women's clothes. My childlike innocence and deep love for him kept me from seeing anything that could have been perceived as unusual, especially in 1970s Georgia. True to the times, nobody discussed my uncle's eccentricities. If it was acknowledged, nobody said a word.

When my uncle got older, he would go out at night. My grandma was not happy about this and would lock him out. I worried about him and would stare out the kitchen window, watching him sitting there on the back porch, crying. I was only eight or nine years old at the time, and I would keep going back to the door to talk to him through the screen. Sometimes I would unlock the screen and let him in, then I would get whooped by my grandmother for doing so. I later learned that at some point, he had cut the screen to unlock the hook and strategically placed it back without my grandmother noticing.

I accepted everything about him; I just knew him as my uncle and loved him. Years later, when he was diagnosed with an incurable disease, I learned that the dishes he had eaten from were thrown away, because people were afraid that anything he touched might make them sick, too. It made me very sad to learn of people's ignorance. I loved him more than anything, and his death would hit me hard years down the road.

My grandmother's protections only went so far. She was lenient about some of the outside dangers that today would be unthinkable, like walking by myself to school. I would walk a mile across a canal thick with water moccasins; I had to climb a rock to get to the top of the embankment, then walk through a dense thatch of shrubs and trees. We called it "The Woods." It terrified me, and I would run the whole way there and back.

For good reason, it turned out. When I was 12, a girl was shot by her boyfriend. The two had gotten into an argument, and he went to her house and shot her and her parents. Then he took her younger, 13-year-old sister, into The Woods, where he raped and killed her. She was found not too far from the wooded area I walked through on my way to school. Only the girlfriend lived.

Along with this terror, I also got picked on by some of the girls in fifth and sixth grade who were jealous of my long hair and pretty outfits. They would gang up on me and try to beat me up, to the point that the principal let me leave 10 minutes early every day. I would run home, and by the time the last bell rang, I'd be making a peanut butter and jelly sandwich in my grandmother's apartment.

My grandmother also couldn't protect me from being sexually abused by a family member at age six. It happened during a visit to my aunts in Atlanta. My cousins and I were staying at one of the in-law's houses.

The person who sexually abused my cousins and me was an older family member who tried to penetrate us when we were just girls. I never said a word to anyone and none of us ever talked about it. I buried it deep inside and never talked about it until I was an adult. When I told my aunt, she accused me of lying, as I knew she would. It didn't matter much, anyway, because the person was already in jail by that point. But I can't help wondering if I would have become a porn star had I not been abused as a child.

It sticks with you. You know that what is happening to you isn't right and that you are being violated in some way you don't have the words to express. It makes you feel ashamed of yourself because you can't help but think there was something you did to encourage or allow it to take place.

Later, when I entered the adult film business, I was not surprised to see how many of the actresses had some kind of sexual assault or abuse in their past. That's what drove many of us to drugs and other self-destructive behaviors. It leaves an indelible scar that you never quite shake, no matter what you try to tell yourself.

It's also horrible when someone doesn't believe you and

tries to say that you made it all up. I felt like my aunt was my harshest critic. Throughout my childhood, my relationship with her was strained. My cousins got into a lot of trouble when I was around; my aunt always reminded me of that and would constantly put me down in front of the other kids, trying to stifle my self-esteem. She would say I was bad because I was mischievous.

Truthfully, I was just bored and looking for ways to entertain myself. Sometimes this got me into trouble, like when I learned to hotwire the Playboy Channel. Other times, my cousins and I would wait for everyone to go to sleep, then we would tiptoe into the family room to watch dirty movies until early in the morning. Being abused opened my eyes to sexuality and eroticism at a young age, and I was both disgusted and fascinated by it.

Regardless of my mischievous streak, it's not good to constantly tell a child they are bad or a bad influence on their kids, which my aunt did into my adulthood; she still considers me an outcast today. I felt like she was my harshest critic. When I was older, she humiliated me in front of her congregation at church. She publicly announced my profession and asked the congregation to pray over me. It was the most embarrassing thing on Earth.

My aunt could be entertaining in a comically horrible way. One Thanksgiving, she got upset with my uncle because the kids were watching cartoons and he wanted to watch the football game, so she picked a fight with him.

They started throwing potato salad, green beans, and macaroni and cheese all over the floor. My cousins and I ended up eating dinner off the floor.

My aunt was very protective of her daughters. We'd been through a lot together as kids, including surviving the reign of serial killer Wayne Williams, who was accused of killing up to 30 Black children in the late 1970s. Some of his victims had lived in my cousin's neighborhood, which had us terrified. We'd run to see the candy lady to buy penny candy Now or Laters and gumballs, then run home as fast as we could. That was a scary time to be a kid, but we clung to each other for survival.

It really hurt me when I was not allowed to speak with my cousins after leaving for California. I know that my aunt was being protective of them; I had had a heavy influence on them throughout our childhood. I would try to call from pay phones in California, longing to talk to them, only for my calls to be intercepted by her. She did not want me to encourage them to move to Los Angeles. I felt so alone in the big city without my family.

Even as a little girl, I dreamed of moving to LA. I saved my pennies, wondering how many it would take to get the fuck out of Valdosta. I was bound and determined to grow up and marry Michael Jackson or Prince. I played their music all the time and can still remember the first time I saw Michael moonwalk. When my grandmother bought me *Purple Rain*, I watched it until I had every line memorized.

I was also obsessed with Michael Jackson, whom I would later meet when I moved to LA. As a girl, however, I was still dreaming of him. Every inch of my walls was covered in posters of him, and even my neat-freak grandmother respected my passion and didn't make me take them down.

Both of the boys I fell in love with in Georgia even looked like Michael Jackson. The first was Demetrious Jones, whom everyone called Skeet. The other boy I loved was David Arnold, who at age nine looked exactly like Michael Jackson with his afro.

I was finally coming into my own, and in junior high, my school days got considerably better. I was a cheerleader and played the clarinet in the high school marching band, the same year our football team won state. I was also active in dance and school plays and I won awards for skating, singing, and dancing.

My grandmother slowly eased her reins on me, though it still was a struggle to get her permission to do the everyday things most teenagers didn't think twice about like going shopping or hanging out with a friend after school. After I begged her, she allowed me to go to a school dance with Greg, another boy I liked at the time, and eventually let me attend football games and perform at halftime. She never came to any of those games herself, nor did she leave the house very often for anything but to buy groceries or to get money orders at a nearby bookstore to pay the bills.

She also didn't talk to me about the birds and the bees

like a lot of parents did, so I was on my own when I finally got my period at age 11. I was so scared and ashamed and had no idea what to do. I tried to hide my underwear, but my grandmother eventually found out and told me I'd gotten my period. She was concerned because I was so young.

Despite my grandmother's overprotectiveness, I lost my virginity at age 12. I think my earlier sexual abuse made me vulnerable to being groomed by an older man. (Also, as much as I hate to say it, my grandmother's extreme caution about sex made me want to explore it.) This guy was 19, which sets off all kinds of alarm bells in my adult self. He lived in the projects and would always tell me how pretty I was and how beautiful my hair looked when he passed by as I was playing on the porch. All the girls thought he was good-looking, so I found his attention flattering. He had a motive, of course, and this was my first predatory experience.

One day, when I was walking to the store for my grandmother, he pulled up beside me and asked if I wanted a ride. Eventually, those rides turned into excursions where he would pull over the car and finger-bang me. Eventually, this turned into sex, which was not pleasant. All I could think about was being ripped apart by this guy, who was much older than me. I guess that's why my view of sex has always been from an animalistic viewpoint: my first experience was not only painful but also meaningless and somewhat volatile.

A lot of things that happened back then continue to percolate in the time capsule of my youth that I can't quite shake. My grandmother was not blind to my budding promiscuity and was right to take action.

My childhood Home-my Mom went into labor here

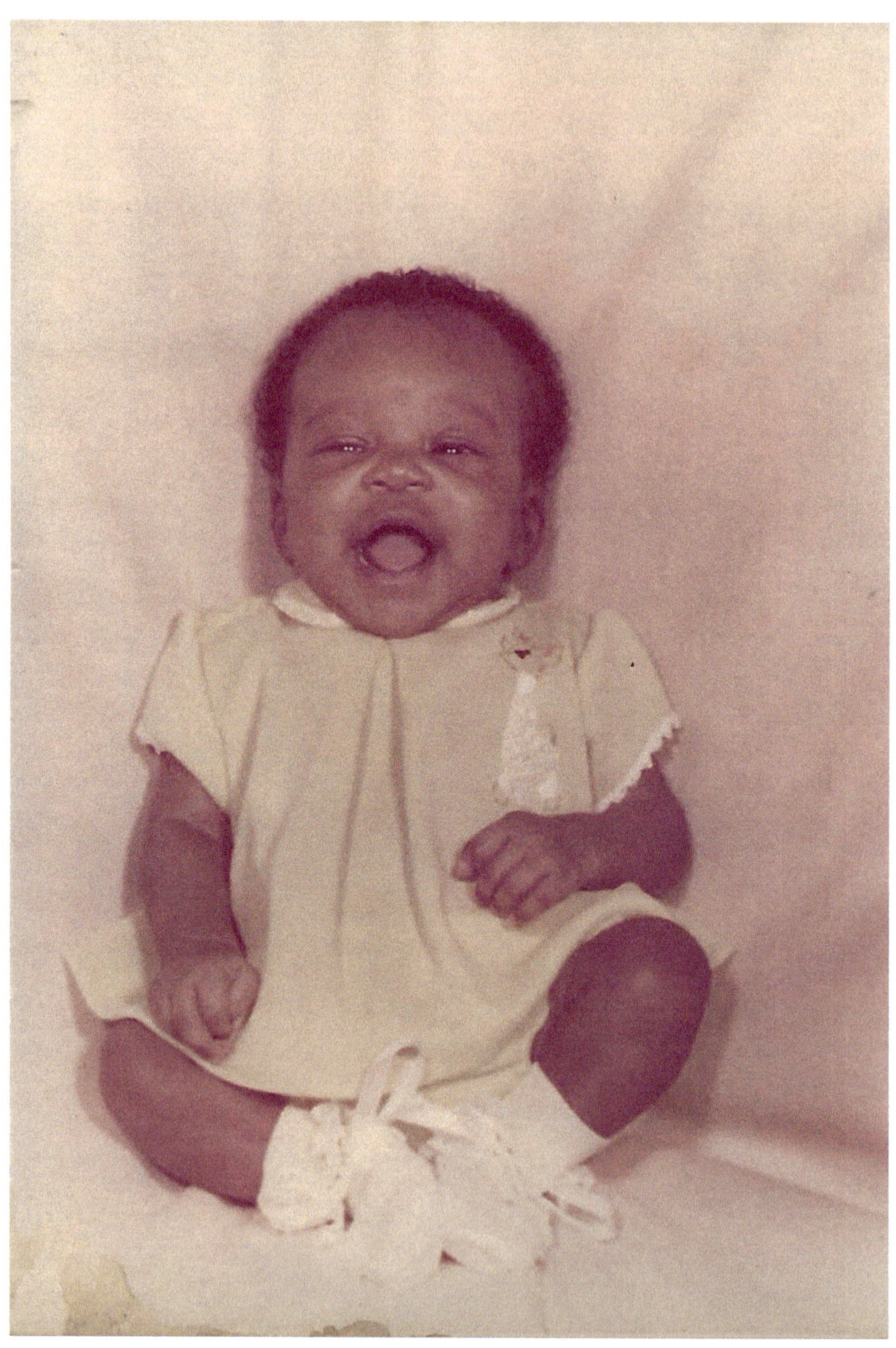

Baby Deirdre

My uncle Jonathon Golden

Me at age 6 in my first-grade year at Pinevale Elementary, Valdosta, Georgia

Me and My Daddy Bobby Walker. He died in a car crash in October 1970.

2

GROWING PAINS

By the time I was 13 and entering high school, my grandmother got very afraid because boys were starting to like me, and I liked them back. Her biggest fear was that I would become pregnant, and she finally couldn't take the stress and anxiety anymore. She called my mom and asked her to take me back with her to West Virginia to live.

It was devastating. I had to leave without getting to say goodbye to Skeet or any of my friends. Later, my grandmother told me it was the hardest decision she ever had to make. I remember the tears running down her face as she stood at the door, watching me and my mom drive away. She ultimately closed the door because she didn't want me to see her crying. I screamed from the back seat. I wanted to stay with her because I didn't want her to die alone.

Even today, I cry just thinking about it. I always had a fear of death as a little girl. I felt like when you love somebody so much and they're not there anymore, it causes so much pain. I still feel that pain. I often dream of my grandmother and my childhood. In my dreams, she still lives in our old apartment, but I can never make it back to her.

I also hated leaving Skeet. I would later learn he had been sent to live with his dad in California. Later, the two of us would live in the same state and have no idea how close we actually were together.

Adjusting to my new life in West Virginia did not go smoothly. On the first day of school, I got into a fight with a girl named Lenny after her boyfriend walked with me to one of my classes. Lenny followed me into the bathroom and punched me in the face, giving me a black eye. We both got suspended.

Living with my mom after all these years was also an adjustment. I loved her cool house on the top of a hill where I would walk down every day to the bus stop to meet my friend Ginger. Ginger was also a student, but she had her own place. I started to spend a lot of time with her and we became really good friends. Ginger also covered for me a lot when I wanted to meet boys.

I ended up getting a job at a movie theater, which was a good way to make friends. I would sneak them in for free, which bumped up my social status. After I quit that job, I got a job in the mall at Silverman's, an upscale men's clothing store that no longer exists.

One day, I saw a sign that the mall was holding auditions for Teen Board to model some of the mall's new clothes. I applied and was one of 12 teens who were accepted, which was a pretty big deal back then. I also took a second job at Burger King, working the late-night drive-thru.

My mother and I, however, were not getting along. We got into a huge fight when I was in 11th grade. I told her I was working at Burger King when I was actually going to a party. She came through the drive-thru that night and saw that I wasn't working. When I got home, she was waiting for me. We got into a physical altercation. She said if I couldn't follow her rules, I could leave.

So I did.

In retrospect, she was going through a hard time herself. She and my stepdad had temporarily broken up and she was really struggling with depression.

Now on the street, I ended up going to a women's shelter. When they found out I was underage, they called child protective services to make sure I was still going to school. The social worker made me attend therapy, where I learned that I could apply for emancipation. I did and became emancipated at 16.

I continued to work my two jobs, model, and go to school. As a senior, I only had to attend school half of the day. I was also able to rent my own apartment. I lied to my landlord and showed him my fake ID that said I was 18. He wasn't much older than I was and worked as a bartender at a spot I frequented with my friend.

The late-night shift at Burger King ended up being a

great way to meet older men. One was a bartender named Kevin whom I met when I went to the bar with my fake ID. I ended up going out with a 6-foot, 5-inch semi-professional basketball player named Patrick whom every girl had the hots for; he was the LeBron James of our time. I started seeing him and having sex on a regular basis throughout my senior year.

I also hooked up with my chorus teacher from school. I first met him at the drive-thru. At school the next semester, Ginger was in his chorus class and recognized him as the guy who picked me up from her house. That turned into a scandal that ended up in me getting taken out of his class.

The biggest highlight of my senior year, however, was meeting Bobby Brown. When I heard he was coming to town for a concert, I was determined to meet him. Those days, when he performed, he would pull a girl out of the audience and sing his hit "I Want to Rock You All Night" to her. Typically, he'd do this while gyrating on top of her on a makeshift bed on the stage, pantomiming having sex. I wanted to be the girl in the bed. When I want something, I do everything in my power to make it happen.

I went to the arena early on the day of the concert to see who I could meet backstage. I ended up meeting one of the workers and gave him a blow job in exchange for leaving the door open so I could sneak in.

As I was lurking in the shadows trying to figure out what to do next, Bobby's brother Tommy saw me and asked me if I was lost. "No," I explained: I was there to meet Bobby. Tommy then asked if I wanted to go on stage and I said I would love that. I also remember meeting Bobby's dad; he had just been in a car accident and had some kind of metal contraption on his head.

Bobby had recently gotten in trouble for pulling underage girls onstage, so I lied when asked and said I was 18. I had on a little ruffle skirt that looked like a cheerleader's uniform, a matching jacket with a halter top underneath, and a pair of heels. It was a bit racy, but it did the trick. The last thing they would have thought was that I was underage. They didn't check my ID.

That's how I ended up being the girl onstage. I was the luckiest girl in the world to have Bobby Brown grinding on me and sweating. He ended up keeping me on stage for two songs. He had some moves.

My mother and her new husband, a lieutenant in the Army, just so happened to be in the audience that night. My mother looked up and said, "Is that Deirdre?" She was shocked I had managed to finagle my way on stage.

Years later, I would run into Bobby and his new wife in a restaurant in Woodland Hills. It was years after Whitney Houston died. I was there with Flash Brown, a porn star and former NBA basketball star. I called him and asked for the name of Bobby's signature drink – Ketel One over ice – which I had the bartender send over.

They invited us to their table and we had a laugh about

my sneaking into the arena and him pulling me up on stage. Of course, he didn't remember that night, but that was a really cool night for me. Life is strange that way sometimes.

Back then, however, being Bobby Brown's girl on stage pissed off a lot of girls at school, and they had a lot to say about it. Rumors of my being a slut began to run rampant, and someone even spray-painted something nasty about me and Bobby on the walls at school.

Luckily, it was the end of my senior year and I was looking forward to getting out of West Virginia and seeing the world. My business teacher knew I had a penchant for fashion and modeling and showed me an ad for the Fashion Institute of Design and Merchandising (FIDM) in LA. The ad was in the back of *Teen Vogue* magazine. She even volunteered to write me a letter and help with my scholarship application. I applied and got in with a partial scholarship through the help of my guidance counselor and business teacher.

I was on my way. Finally. I'd be in California in less than two months. The day before I left, my friends came over to my apartment to say goodbye.

My mother also came by to see me off on the Greyhound bus. We'd just begun to reestablish our relationship, which would take years for us to fully repair. It was a bittersweet moment for us both. As much as I was ready for a new life, I was going to miss her and the opportunity to spend more time together.

She recently told me that she regretted dropping me off at the bus stop. I explained it wouldn't have mattered, because if she hadn't taken me, I would have found a way to California. That's where I was meant to be. I knew it even way back then. I think that much of life is pre-scripted.

I walked to school crossing this wood area

My High School - Valdosta High School

My College - FIDM (Fashion Institute of Design and Merchandising)

3

A STAR IS PORN

People always want to know how I became a porn star. Was it something I always wanted to do, or something I fell into? The short answer is the latter. At the time, I had no idea life would take me in that direction. But like a lot of things, I fell into it out of necessity. I was broke and needed money to pay the rent.

The bus from West Virginia to LA took three days. When I got there, I didn't have a long-term plan beyond attending fashion school. I'd moved with about $28, which I used to immediately stock up on ramen noodles. When I told my family I was moving to California, they told me it was up to me to cover my finances, because I'd chosen to move away. At 17, I was confident I could survive, having already taken care of myself through high school. Being on my own was nothing new, so I was pretty sure I could take care of whatever obstacles life threw at me.

I moved in with three other girls from school. Two of them were white "Beverly Hills 90210" types like Kelly and

Brenda. Charlotte, with whom I was closest, was the only other Black student. The rest were rich white kids and Asians, very wealthy kids whose parents told them they needed to go to school, so they chose fashion. There were only two fashion institutes: one in LA and another in New York. We were at a prestigious school, and the other students were very welcoming to us. There was no time that we felt like we were out of place because California was such a melting pot. You could be on one street and pass someone in their half-a-million-dollar Bentley and go around the corner and see a bunch of homeless people sleeping on the street.

We lived in a very nice four-bedroom apartment in LA near downtown. I would commute from our apartment to school on a bus. To support myself, I got a job working in the jewelry department at Bullock's department store. It was a pretty grueling schedule. I had to get up around 5 a.m., take three different buses to get to school, then work.

As a small-town girl in a big city, I felt pretty shell-shocked when I arrived. The city had two sides to itself: day and night. During the day, the downtown area was this beautiful fashion district with women in nice dresses and men in suits. I thought that Hollywood Boulevard would be all lit up in neon lights like Las Vegas, but it was actually very plain and grimy.

Some nights, going home from work in the dark was downright frightening. Homeless people and derelicts scattered from the darkness like rats. It was very creepy, and

I wasn't used to strange people coming up to me and asking for money. It's nothing like it is today, but for a 17-year-old small-town girl from Georgia, it was too fast-paced and downright scary.

You never knew what evils were lurking in the shadows. I remember passing by the Cecil Hotel without thinking twice, only to learn years later after watching a Netflix special that it was home to transients and at least two serial killers, including Richard Rodriguez, the "Night Stalker," who lived there for a year in the mid-'80s during his reign of terror when he killed 13 girls. Others went there to commit suicide. It's also where the body of a woman was found in a water tank on the roof in 2013. Today, it's scary to think how many times I blithely scooted past danger completely unaware.

But I slowly learned the lay of the streets and began to feel more comfortable in my skin.

Apart from the long commute, school was fine. I ended up becoming tight with Alexis Arquette, the brother of David, Patricia, and Rosanna. The two of us would sit in the back of the class, laughing and joking with each other. I remember Alexis telling me that his family wanted him to do something with his life, so he chose fashion. He was my buddy, and we would sit in class joking about when our teacher would finally come out of his very closed closet.

I also started getting city life and realized how many superstars and celebrities were just within reach. One of my roommates, Charlotte, and I would hang out a lot together and explore the city. One of our favorite things to do was go to see the *Arsenio Hall Show*, which I was obsessed with.

Back in the day, Arsenio was legendary. He'd get the hottest stars on his show, like Eddie Murphy, whom I was obsessed with at the time, and all the A-listers and up-and-coming bands. Once, Michael Jackson made an appearance. I still believe this was the best talk show of all time.

Charlotte and I would take turns waiting in line to get on the show. People from all over the country would get there as early as 3 a.m. to wait for the 300 or so tickets that were handed out five hours later. Then, we'd all come back to wait in line again for the show.

Even standing in line was a party. The area around Paramount Studio 299, where the show was filmed, was pretty dumpy, but the mood was always festive. We loved just hanging out before and after the show to see who we could see. The music groups and celebrities on that night's show would pull up in their limos. Sometimes they would wave at us as they were leaving, and on occasion, they'd even come out of the studio to greet their fans.

One night, we were hanging out when a limo stopped. Someone rolled down the window and invited me and Charlotte to come home with them and watch the show. It was the guys from Digital Underground. They'd singled us out, and of course, we hopped in. They took us back to the Mondrian Hotel. We hung out in their suite, had drinks, and watched the show. Tupac was there and was very laid-back and cool. This was back in the day of the "Humpty Dance."

We also got to hang out with Tone Loc after my roommates and I discovered he was our neighbor. We were living in Hollywood on the corner of Olympic and Curson Street. We'd constantly see Corvettes and other fancy cars coming and going from the place across the street, so we were curious who lived there; my roommates thought they were rappers because of the fancy cars. They dared me to go across the street and knock on the door to introduce myself. I was the one who was crazy enough to do that, so they were smart to ask me.

It turned out that the owner of the Corvette was Tone Loc's cousin, Tony. He invited me to come in and play a game of pool and said his cousin Tone Loc lived there. I played some pool and then I asked if I could go grab a glass of water from the kitchen. In the backyard, a guy was shooting hoops by himself. I watched him for a while and then asked who he was. It turned out to be Will Smith. Tony said he was a new rapper with one song – "Parents Just Don't Understand" – at that point. This was before Smith would become well-known for his acting in *Fresh Prince of Bel-Air* and blockbuster films.

Eventually, Tony asked if I had any girlfriends, because Tone was playing at a club called the Hollywood Palladium that night. I called Charlotte and the two of us rode to the show in the limo with Tone Loc, Tony, and some other guys. At the performance, I also got to meet Coolio and some of the big rappers of the day.

Coolio was the nicest guy, and Tone was also very down-to-earth. There were just nice guys, not the hard-core thugs they presented as. People ask me what it was like to be a teenager hanging out with these rappers. Truthfully, everything happened so fast and there was no time to be star-struck. It was just an exciting time in my life and the start of my hanging out with entertainers.

As fun as it was, though, we also saw the negative side of this glamorous life. These guys had no privacy. When we were in the limo with Tone Loc, we had to sit and wait forever because there were fans circulating the vehicle and we couldn't get out.

After that, we always hung out at his house. There were always people over there, from musicians to up-and-coming comedians.

I ended up dropping out of school after six months. I was having a hard time working and trying to stay afloat and was also tired of the long commute. I also felt like I was learning more at my job (I had just taken a new job as assistant manager at the Limited Express off of Rodeo Drive in Beverly Hills) than I was in school and thought it was easier to go that route.

I was making enough money to survive, and things were going well for all of us until two of our roommates decided to quit school and abruptly move out. Charlotte and I couldn't afford to cover the other two girls' share. I told her, "Girl, this is hard," and started looking around for other opportunities to make more money.

I worked briefly at a seedy club in downtown LA where men would pay money to dance with me. It didn't last long. Later, I found out it was an undercover prostitution ring, which didn't surprise me in the least.

Then I saw an ad in *LA Weekly* for figure modeling. I thought, "This might be cool. I could model swimsuits and get paid." But when I went in, I realized this was no figure modeling job. Despite a couple of posters on the wall of women in bathing suits, it was a bait and switch. The guy in charge explained that they were looking for nude models for magazines. I thought, "I can't do that. My grandma will kill me."

I did get one job modeling: I was the centerfold for *Ebony Men* magazine in 1991. But after that, nothing.

Two weeks later, an agent called me to do a shoot for *Hustler* magazine with a French Canadian girl named Simone. It would pay $500. Charlotte and I had just been kicked out of our apartment because we couldn't cover the rent and were sleeping on a neighbor's floor, so out of desperation, I agreed to do it. I figured it was a one-time deal and that few people would ever see it. I felt responsible for Charlotte because she was in LA alone, just like myself. She had been there for me when I had no one else. I wanted to do whatever I had to for us to survive.

During the shoot, I met a girl named Sequoia who told me I photographed well and wanted to know if I was interested in doing adult films. She invited me to come to the set the next day where Ron Jeremy was doing a film for Video Exclusives, a major producer for A-list porn stars.

At the same time, I was introduced to a guy named Pipes who was connected to the industry. He took Charlotte and me to stay at the beach house of a friend who just happened to be actor Robert Z'Dar, the star of the movie *Maniac Cop*. Pipes drove me to the set. I had mixed feelings about the whole movie thing.

At that point in my life I hadn't even seen a porn movie, let alone considered being in one. In the late '80s, you had to go to the back room of video stores to rent movies, each of which cost several hundred bucks to purchase. It was taboo as far as I was concerned.

My first porn shoot was bizarre. I felt like I'd walked into a dark world. Naked people were everywhere and sex acts were being performed on all these different stages. There were beautiful women with big hair, perfect bodies, and glamorous makeup. It was a wild scene, but everyone was so nice that I began to feel more comfortable.

That day, a famous porn star and director (whom I am not naming for legal reasons) were making a film with a Black actor named Ray Victory and Ray's wife, Jean Afrique, a Dutch nude model who reminded me of Bo Derrick. The couple was getting ready to move to Germany and this was going to be their last film.

The director asked who I was and if I was available for the film. I was shocked and pretty confused, but when he told me it paid $500, which was a lot of money for a newcomer, I started to warm up to the idea. (Some girls worked for as little as $50 to $100 per scene in those days.)

At first, the director tried to put me in a scene with Ray, but it didn't work out. Instead, I was thrown into an interracial scene with Terri Weigel, an ex-Playboy Playmate who had just entered porn. It was an absolute no-no for Playmates to cross over into this world because it would taint their image.

I now consider myself bisexual, but even though I liked girls back then, I'd never been with one sexually. The most I'd done at that point was fool around with a girl in Georgia, but we just grinded against each other with our clothes on.

On the set, I was terrified and had no idea what I was doing. The actual filming was anything but sexual. There were lights and cameras everywhere, including on our genitals, so they could catch the cum – or money – shot, as it's called. We were surrounded by people, including the director, producer, camera and lighting men, and a sound guy.

The director told me to go check out other scenes in the studio to get the feel for what I was supposed to do. I was super uncomfortable and had to take a lot of breaks. At one point, I went into the bathroom and cried because I felt so ashamed. But I also really needed the money.

Working with Terri made it so much better, because she was fairly new herself, and she made me feel really comfortable. I had to learn quickly, though. I had never given a girl oral and did not really know what to do. The director told me to use my tongue like I was licking a lollipop. I was a quick learner.

I pulled off the scene. Charlotte was in the car waiting for me; we went and got groceries.

After I did that gig I thought, "That wasn't so bad. I can do this." The only thing on my mind at that point was survival. I wasn't really talking to my mother. My aunt had all but written me off and encouraged my cousins not to talk to me. I didn't feel like I had anywhere to turn. I knew I had to make this work.

For the first time, I realized I was far from home on my own and needed to figure out a way to take care of myself. Adult films definitely seemed to pay the bills and I decided to give it a try.

A few weeks later, I got a call to work with Henri Pachard, a porn film director.

My first scene was with Peter North, who at the time was the best-known male porn star in the world. I had an instant attraction to him. He had a nice body, smelled good, and had a huge dick. I was excited to work with him, but he wasn't as eager because I was so young. He took one look at me and asked if I was old enough to be shooting films. I was 18 and pretty petite, and he was about 10 years older. Even after we started the scene he stopped because he still felt I was too tight and he was hurting me. He was determined I was underage.

Regardless, we shot the scene and it turned out we had a lot of chemistry together. I made nearly $2,000 for that one film and realized this could be a lucrative opportunity.

Then I met two people who changed my life.

One was Angel Kelly. At the time, she was the premiere African American porn star. Angel was beautiful: she had the body of a model, with very long legs. I was immediately starstruck. Angel had been the first Black actress to cross over into mainstream interracial porn, along with Jeannie Pepper, Heather Hunter, and Sinnamon Love; Janet Jacme, who later shot to superstardom and became a close friend of mine, entered the business after me.

This was at a time when few Black women were making adult films. Angel was instrumental in paving the way for the rest of us and was one of the biggest names in the field.

Angel and I met under not the best of circumstances at the Video Software Dealers Association (VSDA) show in Las Vegas in 1990. I'd done one video for Video Exclusive, and they'd sent me to the show to sign autographs. All of the adult film stars were staying at the Tropicana.

I was going up the escalator to go to the bar and passed

Angel on her way down. She was with her best friend, Porsche Lynn. Angel turned around when she saw me and followed me into the bathroom in the bar. She wanted to know if I was hitting on her boyfriend.

"Who's your boyfriend?" I asked.

She said she was dating Pachard's son Nathan, who had been a gaffer on one of my films and flirted with me. I explained I didn't even know him and had absolutely no interest in him. She was cool. She must have seen the innocence in me. I think I reminded her of herself.

She decided she wanted to help me out by having me play her sister in a film where she was going to be killed off. She wanted out of the industry and this was going to be her last role.

At the time, this was just not done: porn actors didn't retire by killing themselves off in movies. But Angel did. The film was called *Even More Dangerous* – a sequel to her directorial debut film *Dangerous* – and I was cast as her sister. It had a terrific script and remains one of the best shows I've ever worked on.

That's one of the big differences between porn today and then. We had scripts and took our acting seriously, whereas today it's just one sex scene after another. There's no dialogue; women are thrown on a cover just sticking out their asses. During our era, we shot beautiful, tasteful covers and had scripted movies that required actual acting.

Even More Dangerous was a brilliant move for my career

because Angel metaphorically anointed me in her shadow and passed on her torch to me. From then, I inherited her fanbase and my career really started to take off.

Angel and I are still in touch to this day. I have deep respect and love for her and her generosity in helping launch my film career. If it wasn't for her, I sincerely doubt I would have been so successful.

Later in life, I would realize how lucky I was to step so easily into fame. When I entered the business in 1989, there was only a handful of African Americans working in the industry. There weren't many of us, but I arrived just as interracial sex was becoming mainstream.

I think this was the golden era of adult films. It was also a period in which cultures and industries were beginning to meld together. People weren't as judgmental of adult films, and overall, the industry felt classier and less saturated than it is today.

The second person who helped me in so many ways was TT Boy. His real name is Phillip Troy Rivera, but he adopted TT Boy – Troy The Boy – when he started doing adult films. We got into the business around the same time in the late '80s.

He was already a big star, known for his brooding good looks and tireless energy. He was a great performer with a nice body. He was really sexy and looked a lot like Charlie Sheen.

We had the same agent, Jim South, who passed away

in 2020. Jim was like a father to me and the other actors and actresses he represented. Not only did he manage our careers, but he also helped keep our lives on track, and he really cared about us. We were his kids, not just his clients. It wasn't just business with Jim. He was the person I would call when I got upset with TT.

He showed my picture to TT, who thought I was really hot. A month later, the two of us were cast in a photoshoot for Roy Brunington. The photoshoot went well, and TT flirted with me the whole time.

We did our first scene together, then another the next day. We hit it off and there was serious chemistry. After we were done filming on the second day, TT took me back to my apartment in North Hollywood. Charlotte and I had not been getting along; we were starting to hang out with different crowds as our lives were veering in opposite directions.

I can't remember Charlotte and me fighting that day, but when TT and I pulled up to our apartment, she was on the balcony throwing my clothes and stuff into the yard. I went inside; we started fighting, but TT broke us up. He told me to come home with him that night, so I did, and I never went back to the apartment I shared with Charlotte.

That's when we lost touch with each other. I found out years later that we were fighting because her friend was not happy with my career choice, and I wanted her to make a choice between her friend or me.

Charlotte and I connected some years later on Instagram and still talk to this day.

Either way, the fight led me to move in with TT, and just like that, we were a couple. And because I was dating him, work started coming in my direction.

I credit TT for helping me rise to the top. He was instrumental, because without him, people would have probably taken advantage of me. Instead, he introduced me as his girlfriend on sets and told people not to mess with me. He was one of the top male porn stars in the world, and people listened to him.

TT believed in helping Black female porn stars and worked hard to encourage directors to cast them in movies. Back then, there was just a handful of us working, but he advocated for a lot of us. I think that's why I was able to work with companies like Wicked and Video Exclusive, which didn't historically hire African American girls.

Later, when TT left the business to start his own film production company, he'd continue to cast Black women in his films.

He was the consummate professional, too. Not only did he pay his bills on time, but he also socked away about 80 percent of every check. He worked hard. He didn't party and was really focused on his career. I learned so much from him, including his good habits.

He was definitely my first love, and we were together for about two years. As much as I loved dating TT, however, dating another porn star was a recipe for disaster.

We had some serious chemistry. We also had some serious fights. Twice we went to jail. Once I bit him. But more on that later. For now, I was just beginning to enjoy my skyrocketing career.

Beach Shoot

Me In Malibu

4

RISING STAR

One downside of fame is that it's hard to hide it from your family. I wouldn't say I was intentionally hiding anything at first, but there was no way I wanted anyone back home to learn what I did for a living, especially my grandmother. However, the choice was entirely out of my hands.

My grandmother could have discovered this news in any number of ways, but in my case, it was on an episode of *People's Court* with Judge Wapner. I was 21 at the time and had forgotten that this was one of my grandmother's favorite shows when I agreed to participate.

For people who don't know how the show works, the producers look through cases in small claims courts to find ones they think would make good drama. If your case is chosen and you agree to do the show, you get paid something like $500 to appear, and if you lose, they'll cover your fines.

My case was perfect for primetime. My episode was called "The Cabbie Who Got Taken For a Ride."

It began with a fallout with my cab driver who ended up falling in love with me. Before TT and I broke up, I purchased a Jeep with a manual transmission. TT and I broke up before he was able to teach me how to drive it, so I had a new vehicle that I couldn't use. This led to my calling a cab to take me back and forth to the film studio every day. I ended up making friends with the driver, who agreed to drive me back and forth for free if I let him hang out on the set when I was filming.

That went on for a few months before it was pretty clear he was falling in love with me. That was okay until I got back together with TT and the cab driver started to get jealous. He demanded I pay him back for the cab rides and a bathing suit he bought me.

People's Court called me and I agreed to go on the show. I asked Taylor Wayne to come with me as my witness because I thought that her proper English accent gave her more credibility. I warned her to dress conservatively for court (not her strong suit). She didn't. Instead, she showed up at my place with these over-the-knee slutty boots (we called them "fuck me Pretty Woman" boots) as if she was going clubbing. I was pleased that she at least had worn a suit coat over her huge DD breasts.

The cab driver brought his mother as his witness. Judge Wapner got into the case and questioned something I said about the cab driver having posters of me on his walls. The judge wanted to know what kind of posters these were. The driver explained that I was an exotic dancer and porn star.

It just so happened that day that a third-grade class was in the studio audience, and I couldn't believe he said that with all those children sitting there. One of the kids asked his teacher what a porn star was. I was so embarrassed, and I think Judge Wapner was, too, because he was sweating.

In the end, the judge ruled in my favor and the kids cheered.

My grandmother just so happened to be watching the show that day and called me later. I'd been living in fear of her finding out and now it was on national television, for all to see.

She wanted to know what I did for a living and I explained. To my complete surprise, she was okay with it, if not totally accepting. She said she was proud of me for handling myself so well and speaking so articulately, as she'd taught me.

"Deidre, I'm not going to judge you based upon where you are now," my grandmother said, adding that she was proud of the person I'd become. As long as I wasn't hurting myself or others, she just wanted me to be happy.

My mother, meanwhile, found out about it after her husband went to a stag party, where one of my films was playing. Prior to that, she had seen me as a centerfold in *Ebony Man Magazine* and assumed I was just a bathing suit model. She didn't have much to say about it when she found out about my actual career, other than that she wished I had a different job. It was really embarrassing for both of us, and to this day, it's a subject we avoid. My mother recently told me that she was not happy with the choice I made, but it's just not something we talk about.

My aunt, of course, had a lot to say. When she found out, she told all my cousins and completely shamed me. Once, when I was visiting home, she told the congregation at our church that I was a porn star. At that point, she was a born-again Christian. I was really hurt and disappointed by her reaction because I felt judged and ridiculed, but my grandmother's was the only opinion I really cared about.

I learned early on that the quickest way to succeed in the business was to invest in myself. That included my appearance. I worked out constantly, watched what I ate, and hired a trainer. My trainer's name was Charlene, and she also trained Angela Bassett. I trained at the famous Gold's Gym alongside Marky Mark Wahlberg, Ice Cube, and Tyra Banks.

I once almost got into a fight with Tyra Banks at that gym. I had started seeing the director John Singleton; little did I know that he was also seeing Tyra. I made a snide comment to her in the gym, and she said, "Bitch, I will jump off this treadmill and whoop your ass."

She does not play. She went on to say that she ran into girls like me every day. Little did she know that I really admired her. I thought Tyra was a diva, not as big of a diva as Naomi Campbell, but I admired her. I just felt like we were both in a difficult position. I did not know she was dating John. In fact, I was told by John that I would get the part that she actually landed in his movie, *Higher Learning*.

That's just part of the industry and how it works.

I was also really particular about who did my hair and makeup. Unlike some of the girls, I brought in and paid for my own makeup and hair artist for films and box covers. I only hired the best, including one of my really good friends, Steve Erhardt. He did my makeup for a lot of my shoots. I also worked with Alexis Vogel, who worked with Pamela Anderson.

It paid to put time and effort into my box covers. Before a shoot, I would stand in front of the mirror, look at pictures of my favorite female stars – Naomi Campbell and Janet Jackson – and duplicate their poses and facial expressions. When it was time for me to shoot, I was able to just snap into character.

One thing that really blew my mind was that pornography was such an insanely popular industry. Much of it has gone online today, but even back then it was a multibillion-dollar industry.

I asked my close friend Sean why people are so intrigued by porn. He said the answer was easy: it appeals to human nature's most primal urges. Men will go to extreme lengths to satisfy these needs, and adult material provides a safe and viable outlet to do so.

He also noted that some guys – and women – lack the social skills to adequately navigate dating and relationships, so the fantasy provided by the industry can be something of a substitute.

For people with extremely niche sexual kinks and fantasies, porn provides an outlet for said desires, whether it be bondage, sadomasochism, step-mom or step-sister fantasies, or power dynamics. In some cases, it's too risky to satisfy these desires in real life, so many people turn to porn as an outlet.

Sean explained it so eloquently, but here's my interpretation: some guys like things in their asses; they want you to strap it on or dildo them; there are men who wear pink panties under their three-piece suits and want you to beat the hell out of them on their lunch breaks. Some people are sex freaks and hide it every day behind the normality of their lives. I knew these people very well.

When I was making films, I never thought of the person who would ultimately watch me. We were so insulated and familiar with working with one another. It felt like we were a big family, and everyone was just doing their jobs like for any other television show or film.

I think a lot of people envision a porn film set like a drunken orgy: they imagine we're sitting around doing drugs and having sex all day. In truth, there was a whole lot of acting, and making a film was much less sexy than people might think. I hate to blow up anyone's fantasies, but the truth is that day-to-day life on a porn set was a lot like any other job, aside from the room being full of naked people.

The exception to this is the porn parties following award shows. Those are a different story. There, everyone was having sex; that's the funny part. An A-list actor or actress would always throw a party after the Adult Video News (AVN) awards. I remember one party in particular. Everyone from the business was there. Old talent was in the bathroom screwing new talent. I remember thinking, "Why would I come here and screw these guys? I bet that after the Oscars, mainstream actors don't get together and act like this."

But most days on the film set, it was pretty boring. I once asked my friend and makeup artist Steve if he enjoyed being on set.

"Not really," he said. "It's actually kind of boring. It's stop-and-go, and it's kind of hard to get pleasure from something that's stopping all the time. It probably would be better if it were more continuous."

We'd get to the studio at 8 a.m., along with the owners of the company. I'd lug in my suitcase full of outfits while the makeup artists were doing their thing. We'd get our faces and hair done and sit around in hot rollers until it was time to go to the set.

There, we'd meet the performer we were filming with that day, run through our dialogue, and rehearse our various positions and angles; it took a lot of time for the lighting people to get just right. It was hot, and there were a lot of people on the set staring down at you while you pretended to have sex. This took most of the morning, then we'd break for lunch.

There was a catering table filled with donuts, chips, and bagels and we'd generally order out a large catered lunch and dinners from local restaurants. We'd stuff our faces and then we'd get to work

Most girls went into the bathroom to douche and put in a Today sponge, which we'd later learn was terrible for us. If you were doing an anal scene, then that actor or actress would do an enema. We'd all get our hair and makeup touched up and run through our dialogue again. A sex scene generally consisted of four positions: missionary, doggy, reverse cowgirl, and pile driver anal. I was not big on anal and did very few anal scenes throughout the course of my career. I'd heard some horror stories about girls with prolapsed anuses being forced to wear Depends diapers afterward.

The porn sets usually consisted of the makeup artist, who stood close by in case there were any necessary touchups; the lighting crew; the director; and a photographer, who took still photographs of all the different positions. For each film, we did a soft-core version, where they covered up the penis and a vagina, and a hard-core version, where they showed everything. During hard-core shootings, the director would be doing a lot of directing: "Long tongue, open her legs – we want to see pink."

People hovered over us while we held positions for

inordinately long times, stretching all our muscles to fatigue before collapsing. Afterwards, we practiced the positions again for the grand finale, including the pop – or money – shot where the guy ejaculated on my face or pubic area.

In some cases, the money shot was actually a prosthetic penis with a small tube shooting out piña colada mix.

Today, they do what's called a "cream pie," where the guy ejaculates inside the girl, but that wasn't a thing back when I was working. We never used condoms either, though that changed over the years when the LA public health department cracked down; this drove much of the industry to Las Vegas and Florida where rules are much laxer.

The work required a whole lot of faking on the part of myself and other actresses. I only knew one female star who was a sex addict and just couldn't get enough. The majority of us were performing. I mean, don't get me wrong: you do get some type of pleasure from being a porn star, even if you don't orgasm when a guy is going down on you. Yes, it's going to feel good, and you're not going to be able to block out your pleasure senses. But for me, sex is more than just pleasure. In order for me to achieve orgasm, I have to have some type of connection with the other person. And when you are working a lot, doing back-to-back movies every day, it gets tiresome, just like anything else.

People just don't have sex like this in normal life. I read somewhere that the average sex between a couple lasts seven minutes from start to finish, but everyone wants to imagine sex lasting for 20 to 30 minutes at a time. So this is what we gave them.

It's funny: many men were intimidated to be with me sexually because I worked in the industry. Many of them were self-conscious about their penis size and thought that a big dick was what every woman was looking for. The ones who were good in bed actually didn't have big dicks, in my experience (big dicks are actually kind of a pain in the ass), but instead knew how to touch me and make me feel good. Other men thought they needed to be aggressive, but that also didn't work. The way I acted in movies wasn't who I was in real life.

I was really good at acting and genuinely enjoyed my co-stars and making films. TT would tease me sometimes about my moaning, which he claimed he could hear way across the set in another room. There was more to this teasing than I realized at the time, because our jobs took a serious toll on our relationship.

As my career continued to skyrocket, my relationship with TT took a turn for the worse. The most discouraging part was our sex life. Despite our profession, we didn't have a lot of sex at home. Part of it was the job. He worked every day, which was problematic for us because he would not have sex past 8 p.m. if he had a scene the next day so he could save his pop shot. Some days he did three to four scenes a day, sometimes five. He was a consummate professional and worked really hard. We fought a lot because of this. I constantly accused him of cheating. Crazy, right?

Directors only put us together a couple of times in movies because it was boring. Who wants to see a boyfriend and girlfriend having sex? They wanted more drama. We did a couple of films together but mostly we worked with other actors and actresses.

Most of the drama with TT and myself happened away from the set. We were discussed every week in the gossip news.

My jealousy didn't help. I knew it was just a job, but it really hurt to see TT enjoying sex with other women. Mentally, I tried to keep my jealousy at bay, but when you're in love with someone, it's hard to see them with someone else. It was really hurtful. That was just my mentality; I was a country girl and wasn't used to it; it was the way I was born. That's one thing TT didn't understand about me.

It bothered me that TT had all of these rules he wanted me to follow. One night, he wanted to have a three-way with another girl. I had said I would do it, but I really didn't want to. We picked up a girl at this spot where hookers frequented. I was not feeling it, plus, she did not seem clean. I told TT no. Why wasn't I enough? On the drive home, he told me he couldn't just sleep with me alone. He needed some excitement, he explained. I was so hurt. The girl that TT wanted to pick up was trash, but I felt like I was worse because he wanted someone else.

He told me it was not going to work out.

He also struggled with jealousy. One of the hot spots was my connection with Peter North, another leading male porn star of the time. He and I frequently did scenes together because we had great on-screen chemistry. It was just occupational, and off-screen, there wasn't anything going on between us, but TT frequently accused me of being in a relationship with him.

It was fine for TT to kiss and be with hot girls, but he had a problem with my doing it.

Randy Spears was another thorn in his side. Randy was incredibly good-looking and an excellent actor, and I loved doing films with him. We'd starred together in *The Booby Guard*, a porn parody of the Kevin Costner and Whitney Houston film *The Bodyguard*. It was a great film. Randy left the industry when he got married. I recently ran into him at a Rite Aid and we talked about old times and how we would have liked to do more work together. He's doing well, and it was good to see a face from the past.

TT also had a problem with my close friendship with fellow porn star Taylor Wayne. She drew a lot of attention in general. Once when we went out, she wore nothing but a cowboy hat, bustier, G-string, and chaps. Taylor was my best friend and the life of the party.

Besides our jealousies, another issue for me was that TT worked so much. I spent a lot of days home by myself, and I wasn't the type of girl who could handle that. It played into my fear of being abandoned. I would be sad until he came home, then we'd go out to a fancy dinner and I'd ask him about his scenes. He never knew that I secretly watched his films while he was at work.

It was a difficult relationship and we both knew we'd never make it to the altar. He bought me an engagement ring to keep us together, but it was just a ruse for our inevitable implosion. I wasn't even allowed to wear the ring during my sex scenes.

As hard as our relationship was at times, it was also really good. I enjoyed our home life together and learned many good habits from TT, like being responsible with money, always being professional, and working really hard. TT didn't do drugs or drink because he took his career so seriously, which was a good thing, because neither of us got derailed like some other stars in our field did.

Between jobs, TT made it up to me by taking me on fun vacations. We went to the Hearst Castle where we fished on the lake and went skiing. In 1990, we went to Cancun to see the bullfights.

On the flip side, though, we had several pretty epic – and public – fights. The press dubbed us as the "passionate, crazy couple" who got arrested and did shitty things to each other. Those reports were accurate. We did do shitty things to each other, and we were arrested on two occasions.

One time, I threw his Corvette into reverse on the freeway. Then I did it again, resulting in a huge fight and my going to jail. We'd been working at some director's house that day and had gotten into a fight. I was flirting with someone, and he got jealous. He told me I flirted with everyone and that he wanted to break up.

I told him, "You are not breaking up with me." Then I started attacking him, ripping off his turn signal. He finally got me out of the car, and I made it back to our house before he did. There, I took his leather jacket and other clothes and tried to burn them on the stove. I was so pissed that he wanted to break up. A neighbor saw the smoke and pulled the fire alarm. I almost burned the whole place down.

Three fire engines came to put out the fire, and then I got carted off to jail. That was my second time. The first was when TT and I got into a fight and I bit him. They took us in and put us next to each other, but we wouldn't stop arguing and they kept telling us to shut up. Then they let us out at the same time.

We both laughed about that one; it made absolutely no sense.

Two years – and one major breakup – into our relationship, we had our final fight. It was April 1992 and I was shooting a film at the Avocado Ranch, which was a two-hour drive from San Fernando Valley.

That place in and of itself was bizarre. It was owned by an elderly couple who rented the film company space out on their vast land. We set up scenes in a cluster of trailers, and the couple would bring us freshly baked cookies, just like grandparents, while we were filming porn movies on their land. It was an unsettling contrast, but it kind of felt like home.

At the end of the day, I invited Peter to sleep on my couch, because the drive had been long and we were all beat. One of the girls on the set, Teyana Taylor, heard me offer Peter my couch and ran and told TT. At the time, TT was in Sweden doing films. He exploded. Nothing happened between Peter and me, but TT was done.

It hit me hard. This was another person leaving me. I didn't want to be alone. I also feared what it would be like working in the business without TT's protective shield.

I asked him to take me to 7-Eleven. He stayed in the car while I went in to purchase a pack of razors. We went home and he continued to grab clothes from the bedroom. I was screaming, "Please don't leave!" I went into the bathroom and he came in to tell me goodbye.

He said he was leaving the country for vacation. I turned around and slit my wrist right in front of him. He freaked. There was so much blood. It was pouring out like a waterfall. He rushed to grab a towel. I felt like my wrist was barely hanging on. He picked me up and put me in his Corvette. I barely remember the ride there. I kept going in and out of consciousness. Luckily, our place was only one block from the hospital. He carried me into the ER and the staff immediately took over and saved my life.

I did not see TT for a few months. He'd always wanted to go to visit Eastern Asia, so that's where he went. I stayed in the hospital tied to a gurney. They had to call in a top specialist to put my wrist back together. I was there for two weeks. I had no visitors. I just laid there healing, worried I would never again be able to use my hand. Thankfully, the cut was not as serious as I'd thought.

After I was released, I went to Ogden, Utah for the first of my plastic surgeries. TT always disapproved of the idea (he hated tattoos or any kind of body augmentation and really liked my natural size B boobs), so I figured that this was my time.

Julie Strain said a boob job would really enhance my career. I'd met her on the set of a scene I'd filmed with her and Aidan Quinn for a soft porn cable movie. At the time, she was a Penthouse Pet and ended up modeling for *Heavy Metal* magazine. She told me she thought I was really pretty but believed I would get more work if I had my breasts enlarged. Until then, I'd never given it much thought. I was naturally thin and well-proportioned. But I thought Julie looked great and I was fascinated with her perfect breasts, long legs, and supermodel looks.

She gave me the name of a doctor in Utah. Oddly, Ogden was a hotbed for plastic surgeons, and prices were a fraction of the cost of those in California. The doctor was only charging $2,000 or $3,000 for a breast enlargement, which was unheard of in LA. A lot of the Penthouse and Playboy girls used this doctor, so I set up an appointment and bought a plane ticket.

At the time, I had just signed a contract with Leisure Time, and the owner had 20 photos of Janet Jackson on his desk. He had a certain image of the type of girls he was looking for, and so I decided to get my nose done to appear less ethnic and to enlarge my breasts.

What a bizarre experience. It was like something out of the *Twilight Zone*. I flew into the Ogden airport and was picked up by a nursing assistant.

Upstairs, it looked like any other doctor's office with pre- and post-op rooms. Downstairs, where the patients spent the night, looked like a hooker parlor or a resting place for Dracula, with blood-red velvet curtains fastened between makeshift rooms. The doctor himself looked like a mad scientist with white hair sticking up everywhere. He must have been in his 70s and looked like he stepped out of a horror film.

The next morning a nurse woke me up and I went into a TV room where one of the aides gave me a handful of pills. The next thing I knew I was waking up in a dark room screaming in pain, at which point the mad scientist came in and gave me a shot. It was crazy.

During my post-op, the doctor asked me to look in on a patient who had just had a facelift done. When I went into her room, her eyes were wide open, and she was snoring. I ran out of there in fear.

The doctor ended up doing my boobs twice, because Leisure Time wanted me up to a DD. The experience was horrible, but the end results worked. People began comparing me to Janet Jackson and Naomi Campbell, though some Black actresses gave me heat for trying to erase my ethnic appearance. Regardless, after the surgeries, I had no shortage of work.

Meanwhile, TT and I didn't speak for a really long time. He was really hurt by what he thought I did to him and held onto it for years.

Later, we made one more film together. Ironically, our characters hated each other. It didn't take much acting on that one. The emotion was so raw. At the time, I had married an ex-Chippendales dancer, who also worked on the movie. TT was pissed that I'd brought such a good-looking guy into the business.

We didn't speak again for another two decades, went I went to see him at his studio and film company. At the time, I was dating the actor Tom Sizemore, whom I knew TT really admired. Tom was also a fan of TT's, as well as being really into porn movies.

I was really impressed by TT's success. He was sitting behind a big desk at his production studio, the king of his empire. He and Tom hit it off. It was crazy. Tom was a huge actor who had just starred opposite Tom Hanks in *Saving Private Ryan,* but he was starstruck by a couple of porn actors and actresses.

At one point, TT took Tom into his film library and told him to take whatever he wanted. You should have seen

Tom's face. He was like a kid in a candy store and he must have snatched up about 25 films.

I went on TT's show in July 2021, just after my 50th birthday. He's married now, his wife looked just like me at 18, and their family was adorable. It was sad for me at first because I'd wanted this life with him, but I was happy he'd finally found the love he deserved. We spent more than three hours reliving those days and talking it out.

He admitted it impacted him to see me with other guys, and that it was complicated for him to work with me as his girlfriend because he had an emotional connection and he had to be good. It was nice to finally make peace with each other and to acknowledge both the good and bad times and what we'd once meant to each other.

The truth was that we were doomed to fail, and we both understood that. It's good to have the maturity and insight to admit that now, but at the time, it was just the beginning of my unraveling and descent into a world of deep-seated darkness.

5

CRAZY LITTLE THING CALLED LOVE

Have you ever had the kind of love that you thought would last forever, and then when you broke up, it hurt to the core of your being? Like your life has ended, and the only thing you can think to do is find the biggest razor to slit your wrists? I never thought I'd slit my wrists or drown my miseries with a bottle of Xanax and alcohol. But I did both.

It started with Ryan (not his real name). At the time, he was working as a model and starred in a popular sitcom in the early '90s. He was also up for a major Hollywood blockbuster movie but ended up not getting the part.

I didn't know any of this when I met him. I accidentally ran into him at an apartment complex while looking for my friend Helen's place. He saw me wandering around and asked if I was lost. He was the most beautiful man I'd ever met and it took me a minute to answer. He was like a sculpture: tall and blond and with sharp, chiseled features and a muscular frame. I was smitten.

I'd always heard that by the time you hit 25 you have already met your soulmate. I felt like I'd just met mine. Ryan seemed to be having a similar reaction. He stared down at me with big eyes, like a kid with a schoolboy crush.

He was the apartment complex manager's son, he said. He offered to show me to my friend's apartment. I couldn't take my eyes off him. He was like a walking ad for a male supermodel.

He led me directly to Helen's door and said goodbye. The next day, Helen called to say I'd made an impression on Ryan and he was asking for my phone number. I told her to waste no time giving it to him. Later that day, he called and invited me over to his apartment for milk and cookies.

Now, mind you, I'm a porn star. The last time anyone offered me milk and cookies was when I was in the third grade on a playdate. The men I meet do not offer me snacks. They proffer drugs, alcohol, expensive dinners – mostly with the intention of getting in my pants. This was a first, and I found it abnormally sweet and wholesome.

That first date was magical. He shared the apartment with a man he claimed was his dad, and all I knew about him was that he was an up-and-coming actor. I was so enamored with him that after that first night, I moved into his apartment with him and his dad. I felt like I had a family again.

I had my own apartment at the time at The Grand, but I liked staying with Ryan better. We'd work during the day and then sit down for dinner at night like a normal family.

This was during a really bad patch in my life that coincided with the Northridge Quake, when my life was literally feeling shaky. I had just gone through the death of my uncle. I was devastated and still processing that loss. Less than a year later, my grandmother had a stroke and died.

Talk about losing my footing.

I had been dancing at a club in Hialeah, Florida when I got the news about my grandmother. I did a lot of dancing in those days to promote films. I had to finish out the gig for a few days before I could fly home to Atlanta. My aunt picked me up at the airport. She always called me "Hollywood" and mocked me when I called home. She poked fun at my fancy clothes and what she called the "proper" way I talked (by then, I'd lost most of my Southern accent, which only made the gulf between us even wider).

I was pretty strung out when I arrived. I had done cocaine the night before and had taken a Quaalude to sleep. I was coming from a dance performance, so I didn't have any formal clothes and instead showed up in a pair of jean shorts with red sequins on the back pockets and a matching red sequin jacket and black boots. My cousins still talk about waiting for me to get off the plane, and here I come in my flashy outfit with my long hair down to my butt. They thought it was really fun.

My mom, not so much. She had to take me to the store to

buy a proper dress for the funeral. I got my hair cut shoulder-length to match my conservative dress. I was stricken by grief and the alienating feeling of being uncomfortable with my family. I was at such a different place in my life, and I hadn't seen my cousins in a while because my aunt had encouraged them not to contact me.

It was awkward. Imagine going to Hollywood and becoming a celebrity, then coming back to the small town where you grew up. It felt really behind the times and was just weird. I'd always been the black sheep in my family because even though I was smart, I got into trouble in school for fighting and other behavioral issues.

Now, back in Georgia at the funeral, I was devastated and just dragged myself through. I'd lost my bearings at this point. Other than my mom, I had no family anymore. My uncle and grandmother were the glue that kept us all together: without them, we began to drift apart.

In my dreams, I can feel my grandmother and my desire to hug her is so strong. I often dream of going back to my childhood home. Sometimes she opens the door for me, but every time I get close, the door shuts or I can't get up the steps. I know she's standing within arm's reach, but I can never quite get to her. She was everything to me. Her death absolutely rocked me; the realization that I was truly on my own. I was 23 and at the height of my career, but I felt like I'd lost everything. I got down to 100 pounds as my life spiraled.

This was my descent into hardcore drugs. I had been dancing at the Tropicana Hotel in Las Vegas promoting a new film when one of the girls offered me a hit of ecstasy. She said it would make me feel good. Despite making porn movies, I was really shy and found it hard to dance and sign autographs for my fans. It's funny. Shooting films, you don't think about who is watching them. Then you realize that strangers have intimate fantasies about you and pay to have you sign their posters. Tuning out sounded good.

I took the pill and felt the weight of my pain begin to dissipate. It was a gradual decline, but soon, I was hooked. I started off with cocaine, Xanax, and phen phen diet pills. That was the beginning.

Then I started using heroin, speed, cocaine, and molly. Whatever I could get my hands on. I became a full-blown party girl, going out nearly every night with my co-stars Taylor, Mimi, and Olivia.

I was lucky that my drug use didn't derail my career and I never used while working. For me, it was strictly recreational, and unlike a lot of girls who lived paycheck to paycheck, I was always working. If I wasn't doing a film, I was dancing or doing some other side gig, like swimsuit modeling or celebrity bachelor parties. I always had access to money and could pick and choose when I wanted to work and how much money I needed. Having access to money is not necessarily a good thing, because you can always buy drugs and it takes a lot longer to hit rock bottom. It's harder to stop when you continue to function, especially when you're hiding the fact that you're even using.

A lot of people didn't think I was the type to do drugs because I kept it fairly under wraps. My close friends knew because I partied with them, but I also did drugs when I was home alone. The death of my grandmother and uncle, coupled with drugs, was the perfect recipe for vulnerability, which predators use to their advantage to exploit your innermost weaknesses.

In short, I was at a really vulnerable point in my life when Ryan took me in and filled a void. It felt good to be living there. I loved the normalcy, the fact I had a makeshift family again.

I was incredibly happy to be with Ryan. He wasn't the jealous type and didn't stress out about my work or judge me. I was nuts about him and didn't think about looking at another guy. Everywhere we went people, both women and men, would stare at him. He was also cocky, which I found sexy. He teased that I would be dumb to flirt with anyone else when I had him. He would stare at me in wonder, like a man in love.

I even stopped using drugs during this period, though Ryan, his dad, and I smoked a lot of pot. We would watch *Beavis and Butthead* and laugh hysterically. Ryan's "dad" had been a chef and would make elaborate dinners. When I met him, I weighed 117 pounds, but I soon plumped up to 147 pounds (and the camera adds another 10).

This excess weight became a problem for me as a porn star. I'd just been approached by a prominent adult film producer for a huge contract. His office was cluttered with photos of Janet Jackson and other beautiful women. The first thing he told me was that, if I planned to work for him, I needed to get my breasts larger and lose weight.

This stressed me out because, for the first time in as long as I could remember, I was feeling healthy and comfortable in my own skin. I was eating like a normal person and no longer doing hard drugs. I felt at peace with myself and happy for the first time in a while.

The producer said he knew of a homeless guy on the corner who used some type of substance that made him really thin. I asked my boyfriend to find out what it was and where I could get some. That was my introduction to "crank," or methamphetamine.

It worked like a charm. Almost from the start, I immediately became addicted. The crank curbed my appetite to the point where I didn't even want to drink water. Within a few months, I was down to 110 pounds. The meth really helped control my eating, but it didn't hold a candle to phen phen, which I'd used in the past to control my weight. Meth gave me a euphoric rush and made my heart race, which was overwhelming.

The meth also helped refuel my addiction to Xanax. I found I needed the Xanax to balance me out and bring me down from the kind of excitement that feels like being on top of a roller coaster before it drops. I guess the up and down of those drugs was a rollercoaster in and of itself. But it worked.

I got the contract and had even more work, requiring me to go back on the road dancing and doing autograph signings in conjunction with film releases. This is when home life with Ryan began unraveling.

We'd been doing just fine and had been together about two years when I found out he cheated on me while I was out of town dancing. My heart broke. I immediately moved back into my apartment in Marina Del Rey.

I also learned that the guy who was supposed to be Ryan's father was actually his agent and was in love with him. The agent told me that Ryan's relationship with me was hurting his career and that he was being passed over for jobs because he was dating an adult film star.

This was not the first time this had happened. Ryan's modeling agent told him to remove a picture of him with me from his portfolio and had the picture reshot with another model.

Ryan was distraught after I moved out. He came over every day crying and begging me to take him back. After three months, I relented, a decision I doubted because he'd cheated on me in the first place. I was heartbroken, but my neighbors eventually told me to open the door for him because they were tired of the chaos.

We got back together. I had just returned from dancing

in Tennessee and had brought a girl back whom I'd met at a strip club. My intention was to help her out and give her a place to crash while she got her shit back together. I was just trying to be nice because the girl was in a bad situation. This is another one of my shortcomings: trying to help people who don't have my best interest in mind. She definitely didn't.

One night, I had been out with my friend Jeremy Jordan, an up-and-coming R&B singer. We were strictly friends and just hanging out when Ryan popped by my place with flowers. My female guest, who turned out to be a jealous and vindictive person who wanted to be in a relationship with me, told Ryan I was on a date. When I came home, she told me what she'd done. I was so angry that I told the woman to get her stuff and leave.

I called Ryan several times, but he wouldn't take my calls. I went to his house and pounded on the door. He lived right across the street from the famous Roxbury Club and around the corner from the Chateau Marmont on Sunset Boulevard, where John Belushi overdosed. It was a heavily trafficked section of Hollywood. On any given day, thousands of tourists walked the storied sidewalks or drove by gawking for a glimpse of history.

Ryan wouldn't open his door, and I was distraught, mainly because the woman had lied and I just wanted the opportunity to explain myself. I went back to my empty home. The girl was gone by then and it was just me. I was all alone again. It was the first time in my life that I felt hopeless, like there was a deep hole inside of methat couldn't be filled.

In my distress, I took a handful of Xanax and headed back to Ryan's. When he still wouldn't answer the door, I crumpled onto the busy sidewalk. I laid on the cold cement as feet and bodies tromped by. Nobody stopped to help me. I looked up at the bleary faces and closed my eyes.

I have no idea how much time passed before Ryan called an ambulance. They took me to the hospital to pump my stomach and kept me on a 48-hour hold. Ryan didn't come to see me, and it would be 20 years before I talked to him again.

I took it the breakup hard. I missed the normalcy of our evenings and feeling like I had a family. I hated the idea that someone was leaving me once again.

Two decades later, the two of us briefly got back together. I was so excited to finally be back with the love of my life, but Ryan wasn't the same guy from 20 years ago; the guy with whom I had had an amazing Aries-Gemini connection and who played the guitar in a meadow in Paris; the guy who whisked me through a crowd while paparazzi chased us when we were at the adult film festival in Cannes.

This new version of Ryan was bitter and dark, almost demonic. The wide-eyed, sweet boy now donned a Baphomet necklace and was a darkened version of his earlier self.

Instead of making love to me gently as he whispered how much he treasured me, now he told me how much he wanted to fuck me in my ass while choking me.

It was so sad to see what the world had done to him. I wonder what happened to the man that I'd once told my friends was so beautiful and striking that he made women and men stop in their tracks. They said the same thing about Lucifer. The dark world had gotten ahold of him and used him up.

When I broke up with him for the last time, he told me, "Bitch, you better close and lock your windows because I can come in and get you through the wind."

I was still spiraling out of control after our first breakup. Everyone knows that it's a bad idea to get into a relationship while you're still reeling from the last one. Did that stop me? Unfortunately, no.

I met Scott (not his real name) a few days after Ryan and I broke up. A friend set us up. He was a Chippendales dancer. Three days later, I married him. I thought he'd help soothe my heart after my breakup, but he turned out to be a total monster. He was an Italian man from Alabama with a wicked tongue and temper. He saw me as a meal ticket more than anything. He quit dancing when he saw how much money I was making and instead traveled with me on the road.

He was insanely jealous and violent. Once he took my phone and erased all my numbers. He also decided I was not going to do any more porn films unless it was with him. We did one together and it was dreadful; ironically, he played a cop who threw me in jail.

He also liked to beat up on me. Once, he punched me in the nose while we were sitting in his car in downtown LA. I jumped out of the car and a police officer who was next to us arrested him. That was my ticket out. While he was locked up, I went and got my own apartment in Studio City.

One day, I came home and he was sitting on the front steps of my apartment, crying. He'd gotten out of jail. At this point, I was heavy into drugs and smoking heroin; there were pieces of foil in every hidden area in my home. I was a mess. Completely addicted. I really didn't care anymore.

So of course, I took him back, and of course, he beat me again. Sometimes, it's only when I hit bottom that I learn to come out on the other side. But it would take time and many more mistakes and losses for me to finally reach that point.

Crazy Little Thing called Love

6

LIGHTS, ACTION, MUSIC

As my fame continued to grow, I'd done a pretty good job of shedding myself of the little girl from Georgia, but I hadn't forgotten about the music idols that dominated my childhood: namely, Michael Jackson and Prince. Just as I had done with Bobby Brown when I weaseled my way on stage with him as a teenager, I was determined to meet them.

Tracking down Michael took some serious stalking. I mean, the guy was one of the most elusive celebrities in Hollywood, though not elusive enough for a super-fan like myself. I was 23 at the time and elicited the help of a friend of mine who was a reporter at *Hard Copy*. The paparazzi were dialed into celebrity schedules and would seek out places they frequented. My friend told me that Michael went to see his infamous dermatologist Arnold Klein every day over in Beverly Hills. Klein was the doctor who diagnosed Michael with discoid lupus erythematosus and vitiligo and who cut and supplied him with over 200 shots of Demerol, worsening his addiction that started in the mid-1980s.

Right next to Klein's office was a pharmacy called Mickey Fine, where all the celebrities went to get their prescriptions filled. My friend told me that Michael went to Klein's office every day between 1 and 3 p.m., so I set up shop in the pharmacy's little coffee shop, where I could see out onto the street. When I saw Michael's limo pull up to the curb, I ran outside and basically ambushed him.

That day, I was wearing a pair of Levi jeans and a black and pink Playboy bunny shirt chopped off right under my breasts. I thought Michael liked big breasts. He called them "titties." I had my weave in and was looking good. When I ran out of the shop, I completely startled both him and his bodyguards, who immediately ran over to intercept me. Michael vaguely smiled at me; he seemed a little out of it. He told the guys he liked me and wanted to take me home with him. They said that wasn't an option.

He asked me to write down my number, so I did. My life was so scattered back then, I will never know if he crumpled up my number or if he did actually did call.

When I told my girlfriend what I'd done, she said, "Girl, that's some stalker shit."

She had a point, but it was worth it. She, too, was a huge fan and wanted to know what it was like to meet Michael. I told her it was like being in front of someone who is truly divine. He was larger than life. He just had that presence, but at the same time, you could see all pain and grief he was going through.

Something in me identified with his pain that was boiling underneath the surface, and I felt a connection with him that would take me years to fully comprehend. As crazy as it sounds, it was one of the most meaningful moments of my life, just getting near him.

As a child, I memorized every single song by Michael and Janet Jackson. I even won first place in a school talent contest singing Janet's song "Young Love" when I was 12. I was so starstruck by the Jacksons and wanted to be just like them when I grew up. I lost my shit when he first moonwalked and I practiced every day until I had it down.

It helped that I grew up with a drag queen uncle, who helped me adopt some moves. From an early age, I was a natural ham.

I also loved RuPaul and his style. He reminded me so much of my uncle, with the makeup and glamour. I actually met RuPaul while he was performing in Vegas during a Consumer Electronics Show (CES) convention. He pulled me on stage, and later, we went to a club called The Cave. I was shocked when he asked me to go. I waited in the lobby for him to come out in all his grandeur, but he wasn't in drag. He was dressed as a boy with flawless skin and freckles.

Meeting Prince around the same time was equally cool. At the time, Prince owned a club called Glam Slam, named for the second single on his 1988 album, "LoveSexy." He opened the club in 1993, and it was the place to be for A-listers, celebrities, models, and club kids. When you think of Prince, this is the club you would expect, right down to the huge purple dance floors, gold mesh, carpeted walls, and huge Egyptian-style figures peering down from the sculpted pillars flanking the stage. On any night, there might have been more than 1,000 people in the cavernous club dancing to Prince's music, as well as hip-hop, rock, jazz, and techno. It was the hippest and most diverse scene in town and one of our favorites.

When I met Prince, however, we weren't at his club. Instead, we were looking for him at another club he was known to frequent on weekends. Right before we got there, I had been bombarded by a *Hard Copy* reporter asking about my supposed relationship with an A-list actor who apparently had been at the White House earlier with another girl.

Despite the encounter, I was on my game that night as we headed to a very popular club in Century City that Prince frequented on Saturday nights.

When Janet Jacme and I walked in, we were ushered into the VIP room upstairs. A big bouncer-type guy came over to me and said Mr. Nelson wanted to meet me.

It was insane to finally meet him in person after lusting after him all those years on his album covers and videos. Oddly, though, I wasn't nervous, primarily because I was young, at the top of my game, and also pretty famous. It wouldn't have dawned on me to think about worshipping him. I was only 23 at the time and he must have been in his early 30s.

He was sitting in a booth, kind of hidden in a corner, sucking on a cherry Blow Pop. He told me to sit down with him. The first thing I noticed was how small he was. He was about 5'2", while I towered over him in four-inch heels. Everything on my body was huge compared to him. Even his head seemed tiny.

He was a people-watcher and an introvert. That's the Gemini thing. I'm like that, too. I can be an extrovert, out there entertaining or being with people, and I can also be really quiet. It depends on what we're feeling that day.

He was funny and very comfortable to talk to. The two of us sat there talking and laughing at the people as they walked by. Janet was a huge Prince fan and in shock, but she was excited that we had gotten to go up to the VIP room. She was just out there socializing and dancing because that's what she did, way more than me. I was actually much more shy one-on-one than I was in a big group partying and dancing.

After a while, Prince invited me back to his house. It looked just like the club; everything was purple, even the furniture and walls. He even had a purple Lamborghini. I asked him what the deal was with all this purple. He said it represented royalty.

Prince and I had an intimate connection. As I've said, we're both Geminis, and as such, we each have a much crazier twin. That night, he was his shy self while I was my crazy twin. We balanced each other out. Had we both been crazy, it wouldn't have worked. It ended up being one of the most fun nights of my life.

Most people don't know that Prince and Michael Jackson were very fond of one another. Michael named his son Prince, and Prince became a Jehovah's Witness, as Michael had been. The industry tried to pit them against one another and make them adversaries, but that didn't happen. I was aware of this tactic because Hollywood had done the same with me and Heather Hunter in the adult film industry, and they couldn't have been more wrong.

I would later go on to date Vanity, whose real name was Denise Mathews. She was the lead singer of the Vanity 6 trio fronted by Prince. She and Prince were an item in the early '80s, and he was responsible for curating her image as an erotic "nasty girl." She hated it; she wanted to be more of a Diana Ross type than a sex symbol. She had a hit in 1982 called "Nasty Girl," but she left the band not long after to go solo and was turned down for the role in Prince's 1984 movie *Purple Rain*. Instead, Apollonia Kotero got the lead. I later found out from Vanity how this really hurt her.

I met her in my apartment building one day. We lived in a building called The Grand, named so for the white baby grand piano in the lobby. Lots of celebrities lived in that building, like singers Christopher Williams and Brian McKnight. It was a gorgeous building, complete with a dry cleaning service and a racquetball court.

Vanity was standing in the lobby with this guy who was dressed in all leather with dark eyeliner on. It turned out it was Nikki Sixx from Mötley Crüe. I walked by and Nikki muttered something to her about me being a "big porn star."

Another night, I was coming home late from a club. Just as my elevator was closing, she jumped in. She was wearing a white robe, and I just looked at her and told her how beautiful she was. She said her name was Denise and that she lived on the penthouse floor. She told me we should hang out sometime, and the next morning, I woke up to her knocking on my door.

We became really good friends. She didn't like to drive, so I would chauffeur her around in her Jeep Cherokee. One of our favorite things to do was go get sushi at a place in Tarzana. She would come down to my place almost every day, and I went up to her apartment on numerous occasions. She only had two pictures on her wall: one of Prince and the other of Jesus Christ.

We began to drift apart when Vanity got involved in this cult church, the Church of the Now. She was a very spiritual person and tried to get me to come with her. It just didn't feel right, though. I felt like I would hypocrite going to church doing what I did for a living. She didn't buy that excuse. One day she came to my house with a copy of *Playboy* magazine in which she'd appeared several times. She told me that she used to show her body to millions of men, and that if God could accept her, he could accept me. She told me, “He says to come as you are.” And I remember telling her, “Yes, but you weren't having sex on film.”

Despite my career path, my desire to be a singer and performer remained strong. It turned out there was a lot of crossover between porn and music, particularly with rappers. I ended up doing a handful of music videos, including one for Brian McKnight. He didn’t know I was a porn star. When I met him, I told him I was just a girl from Georgia. He put me in the background of his video, where ironically, I played a stripper.

I appeared in several music videos, including Snoop Doggy Dogg’s “Murder Was the Case,” as well as one for Dr. Dre. That video was a trip. I was one of several women in bikinis on the set. These women were hardcore stripper types with curled nails and a hard, weathered look. Their image was very different from mine. These were thick girls and no virgins to the hardcore rap scene. By comparison, I was like a petite Barbie doll. They stared down my DD breasts and 20-inch waist as I hovered in a corner draped in a big flannel shirt.

Later, when I stripped down to my bikini and Dr. Dre got a look at my breasts, he said, “Damn,” and directed me to the center of the swimming pool with the camera trained on my chest. I was so embarrassed, and the girls hated on me. Despite that, it was fun.

Women were always really nasty. It was a problem,

particularly when my fellow film stars and I went to parties. At clubs, it was no big deal because there were so many people, many of whom were celebrities. In smaller settings, however, we really stood out. I remember going to a New Year's party with Heather Hunter and the whole room going silent when we walked in. Many of the boyfriends ogled us while their girlfriends pointed at us and made fun of our big boobs or anything else that demeaned us.

Heather and I ended up getting some bologna and bread from the store and then going to her house. I watched her paint. That was our New Year's. Sounds boring, right? I remember other times with Heather when we'd just be alone at her house, and within a few hours, she'd have a full party going. I loved that about her. She liked going out dancing, whereas I preferred to stay home and party.

It was easier when I didn't deal with all the drama from other women. Once, some girls even tried to pick a fight with me because their man had been staring at me. It was so uncomfortable and made me want to shut myself off from the world. I didn't like being out with regular people because it was often uncomfortable. Want to clear a crowd? Just tell people that you are a porn star. Everyone gets really quiet and they're not quite sure where to look as they try to figure out if you are joking. It's happened more than once.

This is why I really preferred to hang out with other adult film stars and celebrities. I also had pretty good inroads with musicians, thanks to my connection with a famous porn actor from Queens who was tried in a U.S. court on multiple rape charges. For legal purposes, I'm not naming him, but this guy was beloved by his male fans despite his overweight physique and otherwise churlish disposition. Many famous musicians worshipped him and thought of him as "the man," as did Hugh Hefner (he was a staple at the Playboy Mansion parties).

Women were another story. He'd often have to bribe adult film actresses with invites to the famous Playboy Mansion parties and other favors because many found him to be a fat, sweaty, repulsive man. I didn't. I actually liked him quite a bit and was really surprised to learn about all the rape allegations against him. I'd never seen him misbehave with any woman, so that was pretty shocking when news broke about his legal woes.

He'd gotten me several invites to the Playboy Mansion, including the famous Halloween and Midsummer's Night parties. One didn't just get an invite, however; they had to go through a screening process. This entailed sending in a photo that would either be approved or turned down. If accepted, you'd receive a ticket and be told where to meet the bus that took guests up to the house. Only a select few were allowed to actually drive onto Hefner's premises.

I went as a vampire to the Halloween party. I got my outfit from a specialty store called Trashy Lingerie, where all the celebrities purchased their costumes. The place was run by a couple who had been doing this for more than 40 years and basically made the bulk of their profit off their Halloween costume sales.

Hefner did these parties with elaborate decorations and activities, including a haunted house in the corner of his ballroom and a big dance floor packed with celebrities in embellished costumes. Many of the women went nude with their bodies painted. The food was incredible, and everything was free.

Any time I went to a party, I always saw lots of celebrities and musicians, like Scott Baio, Ralph Macchio, Marky Mark, Stevie Wonder, and many others. I never went into the Grotto, which was a big pool full of naked Playboy Bunnies; I always thought it seemed germy, and I never did understand the hype surrounding Hefner.

But the famous porn star was Hef's good friend, and they loved him at the parties. This was surprising, given that this guy was known for being notoriously cheap. So cheap, that despite all his money, he still drove a Yugo.

Along with appearing in music videos, I also pursued a singing career. At the time I was dating the Grammy Award-winning songwriter Danny Sembello, who introduced me to many people in the field.

I met Danny in 1991 while living at The Grand. I'd actually first met his brother Michael through the bassist from the band Earth, Wind and Fire, who lived in my apartment building. He knew I was interested in getting into the music business, so he introduced me to Michael, who took me over to Danny's studio.

Danny was just a kid at the time but had already made a name for himself with the release of the hit song "Neutron Dance" in 1984. That was just the start of his prolific career; he would also produce hits by such stars as Chaka Khan, Patti LaBelle, Irene Cara, the Pointer Sisters, and many others. He also won a Grammy for Best Soundtrack Album for *Beverly Hills Cop*.

Danny knew me from my films and the two of us began dating. I was incredibly close to him and was devastated to hear he drowned in 2015. Apart from his musical talents, he was an incredible man. He'd grown up in Philadelphia, and when he was a little boy, his brother Michael signed with Motown. His mother was an amazing cook and she'd make dinner for visiting musicians like the Jacksons. It wasn't uncommon to see a line of limousines out in front of their tiny apartment, while Danny sat at the piano entertaining.

As Danny grew more famous, his producer clamped down and became increasingly possessive of his time; she was an older, unkind woman who made it clear that she considered me a distraction. I'd often wait for Danny upstairs while he cut tracks in his studio basement. When he was recording, he worked long days and maybe spent an hour with me.

It was Danny who introduced me to famous voice coach Seth Riggs, who trained Michael Jackson, Aretha Franklin, and many others. I met Seth at a party at Stevie Wonder's house. My first impression of him was, "Wow, he has a Black soul." He even talked Black with a bit of a Southern drawl.

When he met me, he told me I reminded him of Natalie Cole. "Why?" I asked, to which he replied, "Because you sing with no soul."

My first assignment was to go to the Ebenezer Baptist Church in LA and listen to their choir.

He told me he wanted to make me a star. He made it clear he only trained chart toppers and demanded I take it seriously. We did vocal exercises and worked on developing my voice, which was getting stronger.

My voice, it turned out, was not my ticket to success.

I had many producers who tried to get me to give them blowjobs or have sex with them. They told me this was part of getting to meet the "Big Dawgs" in the industry. It was one guy after the next until I finally said that I get paid to sleep with people, so why on Earth would I sleep with them for a promise that maybe one day I'd get a music deal?

I'd already gone down that road with Harvey Weinstein, who invited me to audition for *Jackie Brown*. Weinstein was notorious for setting up these auditions at night, but silly me, I thought I was there to actually audition, not have sex with the man. I was wrong. He promised he'd get me more auditions with casting directors, but those calls didn't come, and Pam Grier ended up getting that leading role.

I decided none of it was worth putting out to get ahead. I didn't want to have sex for a promise. The adult film industry taught me to be a better businesswoman, and if the music industry was this sex-fueled, then I didn't want to be a part of it.

I would eventually find my perfect role in the music industry, but it would take me a couple more decades to get there.

7

HARDCORE FANS

Blood. Scabs. A pair of pee-stained underwear. Those are just a few of the odd requests I've received from fans over the years. Some of them were really hardcore. A few could even tell me what I'd worn in the more than 300 films I did over the course of my career.

I started a fan club for myself in 1999. I sent out a monthly newsletter, letting fans know what movies I would be appearing in and where they could find me in person at dance clubs and in-store signings. Fans would also send me letters. I would pick up giant bags of mail from a PO Box and lug it home. There were times when my car was filled with trash bags of mail. I eventually stopped trying to answer all the fan mail because it was only me and I couldn't keep up.

I also had a store section of the fan club where people could purchase autographed photos of myself: $5 for a bikini shot and $10 for a topless pic. They could also order underwear. I would buy panties and bras in bulk and spray them with perfume. Some guys asked that I wear or pee in them, and one pervert even asked if I would wipe my ass with them. I didn't do any of this. I would stick a clean pair or bra in the envelope and ship it off.

I had a male supermodel boyfriend who got similar requests from his fans. They wanted him to pee in his underwear, so he bought a bunch of pairs, stuck them in the bathtub, and pissed all over them.

I always thought the panties and bras were such weird requests, but I guess I get it: fans wanted to experience the essence of a person and have that connection. I always found it really strange that guys imagined women walking around smelling like pee.

Fans could also purchase the outfits I wore in various movies, or they could request personalized videos. This was back in the day of camcorders and VHS tapes. The idea was to make them a porn movie made to their particular specifications. Some wanted a striptease or for me to masturbate while saying their name; others wanted me to stick in a dildo. It was always specific and every guy had their special order from various specific shades of white to black dildos.

Fans also had the option of directing their own video. These were always the weirdest. Some would write out an entire scenario, like having me take a cherry out of my drink or lick a lollipop. Others asked me to say their names or call them "Daddy" as I smooched the camera lens.

They would even include dialogue and wardrobe suggestions of what I should wear, like a white lacy bra and panties with red lipstick. All of these requests came with added fees, and it was a good way to supplement my income, with videos ranging anywhere from $200 to $1,000.

I even sold my own blow-up sex doll. It had realistic big tits and a vibrating asshole. I also had a Domonique Simone strap-on and realistic pussy, which I had my ex-husband have sex with in front of me. There were all kinds of crazy merchandise, which invited some weirdo stalkers.

There was a guy in Philadelphia who would send me anywhere from 20 to 30 letters a week, and he became increasingly angry when I didn't respond. He started off by sending me photos of film stills – always the most graphic shots – asking that I sign and return them. I didn't. This led to him sending me a package of photos of me with the heads cut off.

That freaked me the hell out. I was due to fly to Philadelphia soon to dance, and I was concerned he'd show up and try to harm me. I had his address from his letters, so I turned him in to the Philadelphia police. I figured the police would write me off as a porn star who was asking for trouble based on the way I lived my life, but I was pleasantly surprised: they took my complaint seriously and actually checked the man out.

They came back and told me the guy was well-known to them as someone with mental disabilities who frequently did weird stuff like that. They said he was harmless. Harmless? Knowing there was a guy with mental issues sitting around cutting my head off did little to make me feel safer. That's exactly how crimes get committed against women! Luckily, the man eventually stopped.

Guys also asked me to send them blood or scabs off my legs. Some would get very explicit in their sexual fantasies. There were some really twisted people in my fan club. I shut it down about five years later because it got to the point where I could no longer manage it. The fans' requests were getting darker and darker at that point.

One thing I never got used to was meeting my fans one-on-one. They would show up in droves at the strip clubs or video stores where I did signings. It was one thing to make the films in the comfort of our studio with actors and actresses I considered my friends and quite another to meet the people who watched them.

I remember teetering on my four-inch heels in a microscopic, shiny two-piece bikini at a video store in Times Square with a few of my fellow actresses; there was a line of men that was about two blocks long. It got so bad that police had to yell through a bullhorn to get them into an orderly line. At one point, I thought the glass in the front window of the store was going to shatter as men pushed to get inside, as if they couldn't wait to get their hands on us.

The worst were the guys who brought their own photos for me to sign. It never failed that they picked the most sexually explicit photos they could find — the ones of me with cum on my face or with my legs spread wide open. I understood this was something I did in the movies, but it wasn't how I wanted to project myself in public. I always felt so vulnerable, standing in front of these men with these raw photos to sign. I would do it, but it always made me uncomfortable.

I also had a hard time going into sex shops after I became a big star. Early on, I would wear a disguise and go into sex shops to get my favorite vibrator, the Wonder Wand. It was originally supposed to be a body massager and was sold at Rite Aid for $19.99, but someone got wind of its alternative use, and once they figured out it was being commandeered for sexual pleasure, it was discontinued and sold only through sex shops for $129.

Back in the day, sex toys couldn't be sold in video stores, which were cordoned into sections according to genre. There were specific sections for gay, straight, transsexual, and multi-racial adult films, among other categories. In some states, law enforcement would shut down a video store if they caught them selling sex toys.

This happened to me once at a store in Georgia where I'd been doing a signing. I was the only star there that night and it was just me and a roomful of guys separated by a security guard. The guard would take photos of me and the customers. (I had to bring my own Polaroid camera and film, but I could make up to $50 for a bathing suit shot and $100 for a topless shot.)

It was a great way to make money to supplement what I was paid for doing films. I could make $5,000 to $10,000 in Polaroids alone in a video store over a weekend of eight-hour shifts greeting fans and signing photos. Guys could choose to stand next to me or have me sit in their lap. It never failed that a few tried to grab my boobs, but they would be quickly reprimanded by the bouncer.

The store was typical of its kind, with private booths where men could go watch films and jack off. Sometimes, a couple would come in and have sex in one of the booths. The store even sold a product called Rush, a VCR cleaner that people would sniff during orgasm for an added shot of euphoria. These places were sticky, germ-filled messes designed to fulfill hedonistic desires.

That night, the police raided the store after an undercover female agent purchased a sex toy. The agents came in with guns blazing. They cuffed us and threw us up against the wall. It was quite a sight as they ferreted all the guys out of their private nooks with their clothing in various stages of undress. It was terrifying to be a part of the bust. I was so scared.

The store owner was eventually fined for selling toys, but also for selling videos that included anal and oral sex, which were illegal in Georgia in the late 1980s.

Busts were pretty much routine when it came to signings and strip clubs. Another time, I was dancing at a strip club in Chicago, where outside, people were picketing the neighborhood going to hell. My girlfriend Champagne had just opened a strip club and bookstore in a tiny suburb just outside of the city. Needless to say, the wealthy neighbors were not happy, so they came out to protest the new club. The cops were looking for any excuse to bust the place, and they found one.

My friend, the owner, brought me and a handful of other famous porn stars to headline the show, which angered the regular dancers who didn't like us stepping on their turf. They had to separate us. For this reason, we didn't want to change in their dressing room and were resigned to changing in the kitchen.

Once again, the undercovers stormed in to shut the place down. They busted anyone drinking under the age of 21, and I think there was also an issue with the liquor license, because you couldn't serve alcohol in a nude club; dancers could only be topless. These were the technicalities police liked to use to shut down these types of places. Once again, they had us back up against the wall in our bikinis and stilettos, but the bouncer was able to ferry us through the kitchen and out the back door before any of us could get arrested.

It was always intimidating to live on the seedier edge of things and to directly come into contact with my fans. Like I said, I never quite got used to it, but it's nothing like it is today with online identities and catfishing.At least back then, you could see a person's face or get their address. Now, fans can troll you on social media from the comfort of their basement. People can be anyone online. I imagine the online stud who is actually an unemployed guy living in his mother's basement who only leaves his computer when his mom calls him upstairs to eat potato chips.

Trolls abound, some of whom have even stolen my Domonique Simone identity. A quick Internet search counted at least five different social media profiles with my picture or name. There's a woman named Domonique Simone who kind of looks like me and has more than 10,000 followers on Instagram. I also found my photos on profiles in Europe and elsewhere, and I even found a page of someone using my name and photo. A transsexual man just used my photo in his advertisement in *LA Weekly* to come rocking and cocking. It was eventually taken down, but how are these people getting away with stealing other people's identities?

There are so many people who misrepresent themselves online. I used to get so baffled by that. I did not like doing live video chats because I felt vulnerable being part of a conversation I could not control.

This naiveté left me wide open to being catfished in an online relationship with a Black woman named Misty that lasted 12 years and that I only recently ended. I met Misty on Facebook years ago when she liked one of my posts on a friend's page. She was beautiful, and I told her so. A few back-and-forth messages cemented the online friendship.

Soon, we were writing every day as the friendship blossomed.

Misty claimed she was originally from Costa Rica but was now living in Philadelphia where she worked as a finance manager. We talked about getting together when business brought her to LA, but we didn't end up meeting. She would post photos of herself and her friends working out or eating dinner; she even friended some of my friends. We messaged nearly every day, and I considered her a friend despite never meeting her. I shared some of my most private thoughts as well as some intimate photos with her. She got me through some hard times. At one point, she even tagged the two of us together as being in a relationship.

Our communication began to wane when she announced she was getting married to a functional transsexual and having twin boys. Both of us were busy and I understood she no longer had time to talk every day. We started communicating recently when I reached out to say hi and inquire about her sons, who would have just turned three. She responded right away.

Misty never asked me for money or solicited any photos, but I decided to do a Google picture search to see what came up. Nothing did. This made me suspicious, and my friend suggested I ask to FaceTime with Misty to potentially call her bluff.

It worked. The second I suggested it to her, all of her social media profiles were instantly shut down. I felt completely violated, and to this day, have no idea whom I might have been talking to or what that person might have done with our communications and my photos. I have no idea if they were shared somewhere online or what motivations "Misty" had for cultivating our fake friendship. I just don't get it; it's still so bizarre to me that another human could be so deceptive and misleading.

Times have changed, and the rules aren't the same. The Internet, much as it put the porn industry out of business, is now a breeding ground for thieves and opportunists. By the same token, it's also a way to connect with family and friends and grow one's business, whether that be as an Instagram influencer or an OnlyFans content creator. You have to take the good with the bad, but boy did I feel vulnerable letting myself be taken advantage of in that way.

Like a lot of other missteps in my life, I had to learn the hard way.

α7

8

SIX DEGREES OF SEPARATION

If you believe what you read on the Internet, I've had some pretty high-profile relationships. According to the websites FamousFix and Who's Dated Who, I have been in relationships with Jamie Foxx, Robert DeNiro, Bobby Brown, Charlie Sheen, Emilio Estevez, and others. This list is only half accurate and really incomplete. It's weird what gets noticed in a person's life and what goes overlooked.

It's true that I briefly dated Robert DeNiro. He was someone I cared about. When I first met him, I knew he was a famous actor but hadn't seen many of his movies.

He turned out to be one of the more interesting men I've ever known. I met him when I was 24 and was taking a brief break from adult films. Like most nights, I was out partying with Mimi Miyagi. Mimi was dating a wealthy 78-year-old guy who was keen on partying and had no problem handing over his credit card. She took me shopping and bought me a stunning Hermes dress that I was wearing that night.

The boyfriend owned the Bellage Hotel in Beverly Hills,

where he lived at the time. Living right next door to him were Bobby Brown and Whitney Houston. Along with money for new clothes, the boyfriend had also given Mimi some Quaaludes. The pills didn't feel like they were working at first, so we each took two.

Then we went to a club, Ava's, high out of our minds. Ava's was located in the famous Beverly Center Mall in Beverly Hills. Ava was a Playmate and her boyfriend had bought the spot for her. Lots of famous actors and actresses would gather there. On any given night, there would be fancy cars lined out front.

I was just in the door when the owner came up to me. He said there was someone there who wanted to meet me and he escorted me over to a table with six or seven older, well-dressed Italian guys in dark suits.

I had no idea who they were, but I sat down with them and quietly looked around. None of them were talking to me and I was just sitting there at the table. They ordered dinner while I drank champagne and ate strawberries. I was high out of my mind. Every once in a while, Robert would put his hand over mine and ask "Are you okay, honey?" After a little while, I raised my hand and asked the guys if I could get up and go to the bathroom. They got a kick out of that and found me charming. Afterwards, one of the men asked me if I wanted to go to a place called the Monkey Bar.

I was still completely high out of my mind, so I told him,

"No thank you." I wanted to go home. He looked at me like I was crazy.

Two weeks later, I got a call from Eric, who worked at the Playboy offices. He said they were casting for *Red Shoe Diaries,* an erotic TV series from the 1990s which I was eager to be on.

The producer scheduled an audition and I was ready. I had my makeup done and was dressed to the nines. When I got there, the producer explained this wasn't actually an audition and that his friend asked him to summon me there to meet me.

Robert De Niro sent a car for me and whisked me off from the studio to the Beverly Wilshire Hotel, where *Pretty Woman* was filmed. He was in the bar with a friend, waiting for me. He must have been in his late 40s then and was in town shooting the movie *Heat.* He said he'd had a hard time tracking me down and was amused that I didn't recognize him or know he was a famous film star.

His first question for me was about my parents. He wanted to know about them and if they were well.

He was really intimidating, sitting there at the bar, drinking a martini with his reading glasses sliding down his nose. He asked me if I wanted a drink. He ordered a martini with a twist and I did the same. I was trying to be a swank city girl. The waiter came over and brought us a small plate of nuts. I reached for a pistachio, but Robert said they were fattening so I put it back.

Just as we were getting comfortable, the paparazzi stormed the front door of the hotel, pushing on the doors and windows to get in. Robert wasn't happy about this. We fled through the kitchen and down to the parking garage where he had a car waiting. He made a comment about the paparazzi and I responded, "Wow. That's pretty violent."

He asked if we could go to my place. After a while, he started to tell me I would look so much better without my weave. He told me he liked women who were natural. I told him I remembered when he dated Naomi and she took out her weave for a cover shot on *Marie Claire,* and people talked about that for months. He laughed. I was so young and immature. I had no filter when I spoke and that amused him.

We continued to see each other during the ensuing months while he shot the movie. He really got into character; he was Neil McCauley when he came over to my house, still wearing the suits that he wore in the movie. One night, he came home and found me watching *Beavis and Butthead* and wondered why I wasn't watching CNN.

Sex was great with him; he was very dominant but not too aggressive, which you'd expect from many of the dark characters he plays. It was a fun relationship. I made him laugh.

After the filming was over, I flew to New York City twice to see him. He was an amazing lover. He ended up getting into another relationship and broke it off with me. He told me he couldn't be with me publicly because of my career as an adult film actress, which hurt me deeply, especially when I learned he was dating another Black adult film star in Europe.

I was hurt but not vindictive. When someone approached me and offered a lot of money to do a tell-all about our relationship, I turned them down.

Things have changed a lot since I was in the industry. Today there is less of a stigma against adult film stars. Where someone like Kim Kardashian can go viral for releasing a homemade porn movie and people barely raise an eyebrow, back then it was still taboo for big-name Hollywood actors and celebrities to be affiliated with porn stars.

Publicists work carefully to curate a celebrity's image. They determine whom they date, whom they are seen with, and every other aspect of their life. We – adult film actresses – were guilty pleasures. Celebrities loved meeting and hanging out with us – and of course, having sex and fulfilling their fantasies – until it came time to be seen together in public. Then the publicists shuffled out from behind the scenes to tone down gossip and whitewash any actions or affiliations that might negatively impact the celebrities' careers.

Rockstars were a different story. In fact, it was said that you weren't a rockstar until you fucked a porn star. That's just the way it was. They screwed everyone.

I dated my share of rockers, including a member of Mötley Crüe, whom I went home with one night only to realize I wasn't the only one there. I met him while I was doing a bathing suit contest at a club. He invited me home along with some other women that I didn't know about. They got there before we even arrived. I stayed over with him, and the next day he told me he was married.

Actually, he didn't tell me so much as I found out. I got my period and had to ask him for a tampon. He had one; it was his wife's. I had no idea he was even married. Apparently, he had sent her and her parents off to Disneyland, which was only two hours away, for the day. I thought, "Damn, these guys are bold. There are five or six girls waiting to hook up with him." He was so cool.

I once walked in on Slash from Guns N' Roses in the restroom, the same night I met Axl Rose. Slash came and sat down at the table with me and Ron.

I also dated Gunner Nelson of the Nelson Brothers. On our first date, I took him to see the movie *Boomerang* at a local mall. Gunner was wearing blue jeans with holes in them and was the only white face in the crowd. It was totally crazy, but he was completely comfortable being there. After the movie, we went to have drinks at Casa Vega, where his dad, singer Ricky Nelson, used to go.

I was really intrigued with Gunner and his twin brother, Matthew. I'd never been around identical twins, and they were indistinguishable. They even acted like identical twins. They had matching bedroom sets in different colors and matching motorcycles. Eventually, they ended up marrying a set of twins, who were Penthouse Pets.

I really loved those boys and was glad to know them.

There were so many celebrity encounters, I can't even count. I loved running into my friend Rob from Milli Vanilli. We spent a lot of time in the bathrooms at the Rainbow Room.

The '90s were so much fun. Every day, there was a party, and every night, I was at a popular club before having to drag my ass in at nearly 6 a.m. Mostly, I hung out with my bestie Taylor Wane. It was crazy, because we would get bustled through the crowd right to the front door. We never waited in line; the sky was the limit. We always got free drinks, but we'd hear guys whispering about us being famous porn stars.

Some celebrities like Charlie Sheen openly dated porn stars. The tabloids blew our relationship out of proportion because we were barely even a fling. At the time, Charlie was well-known in the press for his blatant drug use and bad-boy ways. But even at his most inebriated, he still came off as charming and witty. There was a little bit of an innocence to him. There was no food in his refrigerator; it was packed full of Naked drinks. We called him the "mad scientist" because he would mix together several different drugs and it didn't seem to affect him.

The night I met him, I'd been invited to a party at the home of his younger brother, Emilio Estevez. Emilio had just signed the divorce papers from his ex-wife Paula Abdul, and his brother wanted to throw him a party. Emilio, however, wanted none of it.

The rules for attending the party specifically forbade us from dressing provocatively, I suppose because they didn't want to draw any attention to the house or the type of crazy party that was going on. I decided to take my girlfriend, Veronica Brazil, who was a very beautiful and famous Spanish porn star. She'd just starred in a porn movie with John Wayne Bobbitt, the guy whose wife cut off his penis while he was sleeping and threw it out the car window. The penis was found and saved by an EMT and sewed back on. Perhaps the novelty of this drove him to do porn. He did a movie, then got a penis extension and did another.

I slept with John Wayne Bobbitt years later, drunk and mostly out of morbid curiosity about his penis. I asked to see the incision. There was one vertical line going down the side of his penis, but otherwise, it looked completely normal. I wasn't expecting that. I pictured more of a Frankenstein thing. I asked him what he'd done to make a woman mad enough at him to lop off his penis, and he said that he'd gotten really drunk and had been a bit rough with her that night. He didn't remember anything except waking up in a pool of his own blood.

In any case, that night, Veronica had shown up in a nice red dress that barely cleared her butt. I explained that the dress wouldn't make the cut, but she was insistent. And sure enough, she didn't make it through the door, so I gave her my Corvette to drive herself home.

I was now on my own and not too thrilled about it. Dozens of other women were already there, and the place was packed with food. I was nervous to be alone at a celebrity party, so I grabbed a bottle of Grey Goose and started downing drinks. It wasn't a great idea. I ended up getting pretty hammered and walking directly into a glass sliding door. I whacked my head and was totally embarrassed, so I slinked out of the room to get my shit together.

I wandered upstairs and ended up in a bedroom.

The first thing I saw was this huge photo of a Black guy on the wall. When I walked into the bathroom, I found Emilio sitting on the closed toilet seat. When Charlie came up and found us together in the bathroom, he told me to stay with him and keep him company. He took off in a limo with a handful of women to go to a strip club. Charlie asked if I wanted to join, but I declined.

I sat down on the edge of the Jacuzzi bathtub and asked Emilio if he wanted a drink from my bottle of Grey Goose. He was really sad and actually crying. He said he had no interest in the party and hadn't been downstairs the whole time. We just sat in the bathroom as he talked about his marriage. He told me that Paula had gone to see a psychic who told her the marriage would never work out between them because he was a Sagittarius and she was a Gemini.

I told him I was also a Gemini and he seemed pretty cool to me.

We got gloriously drunk and began laughing and sharing stories. He told me about how Paula wanted to have kids with him, but he already had three kids from a prior marriage. He said he wasn't ready to have more kids. I asked about the big Black guy on the wall and he explained it was his great, great-grandfather, who was Cuban. He said his dad, Martin Sheen, changed his last name in the '60s because of racism in the movie industry. Emilio decided to keep his last name out of respect for his Cuban heritage.

We polished off the bottle and one thing led to another and we ended up having glorious drunken sex. It was probably the best sex I've ever had in my life, and that's saying something. It was so crazy that I even popped one of the colored contacts out of my eye. Afterwards, we fell asleep and when we went downstairs in the morning everyone was gone. It must have been about 4 a.m.

It was a really nice night. Later, we took his dog for a walk on the beach. I stayed there until the afternoon when he sent me home in a limousine. Emilio later found my contact on his floor and put it in a case with solution that he sent over to my house with his driver. It was a one-hour drive each way. It was such a sweet gesture. We ended up talking on the phone for several hours later that night.

I was over at my friend Steve's house, where Veronica dropped off my car. When I got there, he said some woman had called for me. She'd left a number, so I gave her a call back. The woman didn't introduce herself but said that

Emilio had a Disney movie coming out and that she would pay me to stay away from him. I asked her who she was and how she got my number. She never did say, only that I should never contact Emilio again. To this day, I have no idea who this lady was or how she found out about me. When I went to call Emilio's cell and home phone numbers, both had already been changed.

That's the way things work in Hollywood. Someone in the press must have seen us when we were out with his dog on the beach and known I stayed at his house overnight.

That was probably the first time that I'd ever felt less-than because of my occupation. People in Hollywood really looked down on actors and actresses in our industry. It happened a lot, and it was almost impossible to transition from adult films to mainstream movies and television. Even Traci Lords went on to do *Roseanne*, but she could never really lose the title of ex-porn star. Today, it's different, and there are many porn stars who have crossed over and are recognized as legitimate actresses, such as Sasha Grey from *Entourage* or Chloe Cherry from *Euphoria*. But at the time, this hurt, because the label stuck with me.

This wasn't the only time that someone asked me to go away. The other was an American actor and teen heartthrob who made a series of blockbuster films in the '80s and who also suffered from very public drug abuse and other scandals.

I met him at a porn star boxing match – yes, this was a

thing – right around the time TT and I had broken up for good. TT was boxing that night, so I wanted to be there to support him even though we were no longer together.

I saw the actor sitting in the stands making out with porn actress Nikki Dial. He saw me and left her, and soon the two of us were making out in public. We started dating and went on to do a music video together called "Freak of the Week" with Ron Jeremy and DJ Polo.

Not long after the make-out session, I was called in for an audition. The casting agent explained she was the young actor's mother. She wanted to know if we were dating and if we could please cut back on the public displays of affection. It wasn't good for his image, she explained.

Later, one of my friends invited me to a party at his house. By then, he'd gotten married, but I didn't know that at the time. When we walked in, he was having sex with his wife and other people. I left immediately.

I also had a brief encounter with Jamie Foxx, but it was just that: an encounter. I met him at a 24-hour burger place called Larry Parker's where everyone would go after the clubs closed. They named the burgers after famous celebrities. Once, Jamie saw me and came over to ask me what I did for a living. I told him I cleaned houses. I have no idea what made me say that.

I saw him for the second time when I tried out to be a Fly Girl on *In Living Color* with my friend Janet Jacme. It's safe to say that the audition did not go well; it was more like a big-ass disaster. I am not a good dancer. I can dance white-girl-sexy, but in the Black girl world, I'm terrible. I went to audition as a Fly Girl when I wasn't that fly.

By the time I finished dancing, Jamie and Rosie Perez were laughing so hard they almost tipped their chairs backward. Everyone was laughing. It was completely embarrassing. That's the closest to *In Living Color* that I came, though it wasn't a total wash. After my audition, I was retelling the story to an adult film producer who found it hysterical.

I told him, "Baby don't have back." We ended up doing adult film spin-offs for both "Baby Got Back" and *In Living Color*.

This was the start of adult films crossing over with mainstream movies and television. The shows were wildly popular because people found them funny. We piggybacked on those movie releases when they were at the height of their popularity.

I met Jamie right after my "audition" with the teen idol's mother. My friend Mimi asked me to dance at a bachelor party with her. The guys wanted some girl-on-girl action. It turns out that Jamie was at the party with a group of rappers and actors. For some reason, he was walking around swinging a large black dildo. He recognized me from my audition and came over to talk to me.

My friend Janet hadn't been too bad, but my performance was pretty epic. He'd never forget it, he said. Given my dancing skills – or lack thereof – he wanted to know what prompted me to audition in the first place. I told him I thought I was pretty enough to make the cut, which made him laugh harder. Just the idea that I would try out was funny to him, and he liked my spunk. We spent the night together and that was pretty much it. It was one crazy night, though.

There were lots of these encounters during those heavily intoxicated days and nights when I went club hopping pretty much every night with Taylor Wayne, Janet, and Mimi, at places like the Roxbury, Glam Slam, and the Rainbow Room. There was always a party somewhere and plenty of drugs and alcohol to go around.

There are too many stories to recount about my celebrity run-ins and other encounters, but some of them stick out, like Dennis Rodman, whom I met one night at a club when I was out with my friend Olivia. This was right after his divorce from Carmen Electra. He was performing at a nightclub. The party was winding down, so Olivia and I were called up on stage and started singing with him. It was apparent that he had always had an ambition of being a rock star.

He invited us back to his place, so Olivia and I got into his limo with him. Little did we know he also had a tour bus that he had loaded up with people to bring back to his place in Newport. The tour bus got there before we did. The second we got out of the limo, there were cops everywhere and Rodman's bodyguard told us to keep walking as the police slapped cuffs on him.

The police ticketed him for bringing that bus full of people back to his neighborhood. He lived right on the beach and the houses were close enough together to be a nuisance. People were on the beach drinking and doing drugs.

We hustled into the house, and it was even stranger inside. We were escorted up to another floor where there was this room with birds that belonged to Carmen Electra. All I could hear were the chirps and squawks of birds. She had all these exotic birds everywhere.

The crowd was even wilder; there was a little bit of everyone in there from transsexuals to gay and straight people. I lost Olivia somewhere there in the mix and ended up feeling quite woozy. I asked the security guard if he could take me home. I remember asking Dennis if he was on drugs and he denied it. Later, he would do a stint on a celebrity rehab program as Tom Sizemore's roommate.

Of all my loves, Tom Sizemore remains right up there at the top of the list. Unlike other celebrities, Tom had no problem dating adult film actresses. The guy already had quite the reputation, given his connection with Heidi Fleiss, who later went to prison. Supposedly, Tom was the muscle who beat up guys who didn't pay for Heidi's girls. The two briefly dated, and he spent six months in jail for beating up Heidi at a posh Beverly Hills hotel.

Tom struggled with addiction. He was in jail from 2007 to 2009 for probation violations related to his raging cocaine and methamphetamine addiction. He again found himself in trouble with the law for alleged drug possession and appeared on two star-reality shows about being in rehab with other celebrities.

I didn't know any of this when I was introduced to him, but it didn't make a difference. People had been trying to connect us for years because apparently, I was his favorite adult film star.

The first time I met him, he had sex with my assistant while I was in the bathroom. I'd gone to his apartment to meet him and brought my assistant along. She also thought he was hot. He took advantage of that. When I came back into the room and started to leave, he stopped me and sent the other woman home. I didn't hold it against her; he was a total sex addict and he couldn't help himself.

We were off and on together for years. He asked me to marry him on social media, but I said no. He was a smart guy. I could sit up for hours and talk to him. He had the craziest stories.

I remember one time I was blowing up his phone over an argument. He was on the East Coast visiting his dad, who was a professor and very well-spoken. He gave the phone to his dad, who told me I seemed like an intelligent woman, and if Tom made me so angry, why on Earth did I keep calling? I was dumbfounded, but he had a point.

How do I explain it? Our relationship was fueled by hot, explosive sex.

I was devastated to learn that he had a brain aneurysm

on February, 18, 2023. A friend called me to see if I had heard the news. I hadn't, so I messaged him immediately but got no response. Less than a week later, it was stated that an end-of-life decision was imminent.

We had just been in contact and he'd agreed to write a blurb for my book. I was in denial about his death because Tom was such a strong presence in my life. He had overcome so much. I was with him a few times when security showed up at his home and carted him away to rehab. I could not believe that he was gone.

It pained me to think I was not there as he was fighting for his life. I just kept messaging him over and over. No answer. It was so heartbreaking to think I would never again sit with him in his bathroom while he took a bath.

I miss his stories. He had good ones, including from his work in movies. Tom was in the *Saving Private Ryan* with Vin Diesel and Tom Hanks. He said that in a Steven Spielberg film, you always stuck to your lines. When they started filming, Tom said that Vin was excited because he had a bunch of lines. He was so happy to be chosen for the film, and Tom was mentoring him. But he wouldn't heed Tom's advice. Vin kept trying to change a line against the advice of his co-stars.

Tom also really took pride in his appearance and liked to pamper himself. He loved taking baths with salts and going to Rite Aid in the middle of the night to get his products. Sometimes we'd go up and down aisles as he picked out products for his face. I'm not talking Oil of Olay or the male version of that; I'm talking about expensive face gels and body lotions.

Once, we were in Rite Aid late at night. We stuck out like a sore thumb. I was driving my Lamborghini. He hopped out and ran in to get all of these beauty supplies while the security guard and a bunch of other people chased him trying to get his autograph and photo. It was hilarious. At the time, I was going through my shit with the Department of Children and Family Services, and I told him that it didn't look good for me to be at Rite Aid in the middle of the night buying beauty supplies with Tom Sizemore.

There were many funny times with Tom, but that man really loved his Rite Aid. Some days he would call me and say, "Hey, Domonique. Can you come and get me so we can go to Rite Aid?" We did this more nights than I can count.

One night, we were at the Rite Aid and I ran into a friend of mine. She was pretty and had big tits. Tom wanted to bring her home with us. I told him she already had a boyfriend. He said, "I don't give a fuck. Bring him with us."

We ended up going back to her house. For some reason, she had this gas mask she'd gotten from a sex shop. Tom put on the mask and told her, "You got some big ass titties and sound like the guy from *Silence of the Lambs*.'"

Another night, Tom had invited me over to his place, but I said I couldn't come. Later, though, I changed my mind and showed up. Tom lived in a really expensive condo in downtown LA. His security would let me in when I showed up in my white Lamborghini. They loved the car and would buzz me up without contacting him first.

When I knocked on his door, I could hear people scurrying inside as if trying to hide. I knew he had women in there with him. I acted like I was leaving and waited five minutes before going back. This time I pounded on the door. Tom got so scared that he jumped out of his second-floor window and landed on the pavement. He hurt his hip, and he said that from that point forward, he was only able to have sex sideways; he always blamed me for that.

Sometimes it was hard to discern the man from the actor, but I deeply loved him and miss him greatly. He was a man who struggled with his addiction. Once, I remember being at his house when his door flung open and three military-type men bounded in. They looked like the secret police. Tom got out of the shower and the men told him to grab his pants and come with them.

The guys explained that they were sick of Tom and his shenanigans, and they were there to take him to rehab in Palm Springs. His agent had sent them there. They wouldn't even let him grab a bag because they were afraid he'd dip into his stash. He went off with these guys as if he was a hostage.

I didn't hear from him again for about a month. Then one day I got a call from him telling me he was just up the street from my house. I told him that I was sober, and he said not to worry about it. We could watch a movie and order in some Chinese. He pulled up to my house in his Dodge Charger, one of the few times I'd ever seen him behind the wheel. I opened up the door, and he said, "Bitch where's the pipe. I know you got one, and if you don't, I'm going to the pipe store to get one." His addiction pretty much ruled his life.

He was also really into spray tans. He asked me to go with him one time, and the girl behind the counter had a real attitude toward him. I asked Tom if he'd fucked her. He said, "I don't know. Maybe."

When he was done with the tan, he looked orange. He asked how he looked, and I told him he looked like a fucking carrot. We laughed so much and joked so much about so many things.

He used to tell me, "Dominique, you got some good pussy because there are no other Black bitches driving Lamborghinis around here."

Another pivotal person in his life was another African American woman named Monroe. He'd dated her for a long time, and the two remained close friends. The three of us hung out often. She was a real presence in his life. If he wanted to clear people out of his house, he'd give her a call and she'd come over and get everyone's shit in a row.

I spoke to Monroe when Tom went into the hospital. She said she'd been there to visit him and told him that he needed to wake up because he owed her money.This was an ongoing joke between us because Tom would always say, "Don't fuck with Monroe and her money." Their relationship was highlighted on many episodes of *Celebrity Rehab*. The fans loved their turbulent and sometimes comical fights.

That's the thing with Tom. He loved and fought with great ferocity. In my last message from him about two months before he died, he'd shared his love for me.

"I always felt we were on the verge of the greatest orgasm in my life's history," he said with a laugh emoji. "Because the air around us was, for me, just overcharged. You know what I'm trying to say? And I do mean a physical orgasm, but I also mean a spiritual orgasm that was pulling itself together, as if I'd be able to see my past and my future with no fear because I was with the woman of my dreams."

I told him I loved him so much, and we promised to get together soon. That was how we said goodbye. He was one of the true loves of my life.

9

DANCING WITH THE DEVIL

Imagine a door closing behind you and you have no means to escape. You feel hopeless because no one knows where you are. Then, you're drugged and repeatedly forced to participate in the most demeaning sex acts. After a while, the faces of the men are no longer human: they're demons taking pleasure in hurting and humiliating you.

This is a scene from the movie *Apartment 407,* and it makes my skin crawl. The movie is loosely based on a true story about a fitness instructor who, against her better judgment, goes to a seedy apartment in downtown LA after a guy claiming to be a modeling agent invites her for an interview. She's then abducted, drugged, and held captive as a sex slave; for three days, she's raped by various high-paying clients. She ends up escaping and saving her life, but not without great mental anguish and a sense of darkness she never knew existed.

Those are the lingering after-effects – that despite the otherwise happy ending – a person still can't shake.

I know this feeling well. My heart races when that door shuts and locks behind her.

For several years after leaving the film industry, I worked as an escort. First for Madame Alex, then Heidi Fleiss, and finally, for my friend and makeup artist who called himself Madame Naomi.

Escorting was never anything I set out to do. In fact, the very thought of having sex with strangers – not actors on a set – was frightening to me initially. As with other decisions I've made in my life, however, the money got the best of me. The work paid well, and I was assured that the clients were carefully vetted, and the other escorts were college students, aspiring actresses, or fellow porn stars. In other words, it felt like a less tawdry way to sell one's body.

I want to make a huge distinction here between sex trafficking and working as an escort. These experiences are in no way interchangeable. In my day, I had no idea that sex trafficking existed. I am sure it was there, but we never thought of ourselves as being exploited because the money we earned went to us and we had the freedom to turn down a job or quit whenever we wanted. We also didn't feel like we were taking risks because our clientele was among the rich and famous. We went on our own accord, unlike the thousands of trafficking victims who are being exploited at the hand of someone else.

Technology has changed the face of the game. When I worked as an escort, there was no easy access to social media or the Internet, which I believe has enabled traffickers to thrive. Business at the time was conducted strictly with a black book and phone calls.

Nevertheless, there were similarities in terms of risk that at the time I was too naïve to really consider, though the dangers were definitely there. Any time you walked into a strange house or room, you never were entirely certain what might happen or whether you'd make it out alive. When someone closed a door behind you, you were dancing with the devil, because you never knew who was on the other side or what they might be capable of.

Even as high-paid escorts, we weren't immune to dangers or darkness. What I learned firsthand is that rich white guys can be pretty dark and depraved.

I got my first escort job for Madame Alex when I was 18, still early in my film career. My college roommate Charlotte and I had been invited to a party by a guy named Pipes at Eddie Murphy's house after being audience members for the *Arsenio Hall Show*. I was such a big fan of Eddie Murphy's at the time, so I was absolutely thrilled to get the invitation. At the party, I literally ended up running into him when I was coming out of the bathroom: I smacked into his chest and spilled my drink. I felt like a total ass, but he was cool about it. His house had once belonged to Cher and it was positively stunning.

It turned out Pipes was basically a pimp, but I had no idea at the time. I thought he was just a nice guy introducing me to people. By today's standards, he'd be considered the Ghislaine Maxwell to Jeffrey Epstein. That night, he introduced me to an older woman named Elizabeth Adams, better known as Madame Alex and other aliases she used over the course of her very lucrative career.

Madame Alex was the chubbier, older precursor to Heidi Fleiss. In fact, Heidi worked for Alex before branching off on her own when Alex got arrested. Madame Alex died in July 1995 at age 60, but in her heyday, she was considered the "Mother Superior of prostitution" and was one of the wealthiest women in the world. Like Fleiss, Madame Alex was well known for her exclusive black book containing the names of some of the most powerful and influential men, and she ran her international prostitution network from her four-poster bed in her Beverly Hills mansion. When Heidi became more successful than Madame Alex, it caused a deep-rooted bitterness between them.

The night I met her, Madame Alex told me she was looking for new girls. I am not sure how many women were working for her at that time, but I ended up doing a few jobs for her.

Going to Madame Alex's house was a trip. She called me up to her bedroom where she sat on her comfy four-poster bed flanked by pillows and at least a dozen cats. The cats were eating raw shrimp off cobalt blue and white china plates on her bed. She was chunky and wearing a long nightgown like an older woman would wear. There was absolutely nothing sexy about it, which surprised me. It felt like being pimped out by your grandmother. Nobody would suspect her of being a madame.

My first escort gig for Alex was at the home of a well-known film producer who had recently been divorced. I'm not naming any of the men I met during my years as an escort to protect their anonymity.

The older white film producer lived in a museum-like mansion filled with beautiful portraits and expensive art. There was a cookie jar full of cocaine next to his bed. He didn't want to have sex with me but instead asked me to swim naked in his pool while he watched. I didn't know how to swim, I told him, but I got in the water and kind of splashed around. I have no idea if he masturbated while he watched me or what, but when I got out of the pool, he said that I should come to his house for lessons three times a week. I thought not.

Madame Alex also sent me to the home of a famous band member from a popular British punk band. After that, I didn't do another escort job until I left the film industry at age 27 and started working for Heidi Fleiss.

I met Heidi in the bathroom at Ava's nightclub in the Beverly Hills Shopping Center. This was the same night I was introduced to Robert DeNiro. Heidi saw me and told me I was pretty, then asked for my number and gave me her card. I thought she seemed kind of scatterbrained but otherwise cool.

Again, the money got the better of me and I decided to turn to escorting after I left the adult film world.

I was told that the process was safe. Clients had to go through a strict vetting process and verify that the name of their license matched that of their credit card. It was a good way to weed out the serial killer types because they couldn't afford to pay the big bucks or use their legitimate names. That made me feel safer; it didn't seem as sketchy as I'd once thought.

I also liked that Madame Alex and Heidi knew all their clients well and had long-standing relationships with them. Sometimes, an escort might just do a dinner date, rather than sex.

A girlfriend of mine from the adult film business invited me along on a gig with her one night to see how it worked. It wasn't bad, and the money was really good, so I decided to give it a try.

The rules were simple: you weren't allowed to talk about yourself or share any personal information unless asked. You weren't supposed to ask anything about the client unless they brought it up. You weren't allowed to exchange phone numbers. You were to be their date and do whatever they wanted, within reason.

Most of the guys were really cordial and decent, and some even showed me photos of their wives and girlfriends after we were done. It always shocked me, because those women were so beautiful. I'd ask them why they wanted to be with someone else, and the answers were always the same. Either the women wouldn't give oral sex or they never listened to them. Mostly, these guys were lonely and wanted to be heard.

Others had a deeper, darker side that they didn't want to share with their intimate partners. They wanted a nameless, faceless person to fulfill their (sometimes) twisted fantasies. When men paid for sex, most of them were exercising the kinky sides that their wives or girlfriends wouldn't tolerate. Some of these guys were perverts at heart, and some were downright frightening. Some of the requests – like being peed or pooped on and other gross stuff – were just weird. Up until then, I had no idea that people with power and money could be twisted.

In fact, the wealthier the man, the more depraved he seemed to be, and I met several of those during my escort years. It makes sense when you think about it. These really accomplished men have everything they want, so they're always pushing for new experiences. The more they succeed, the more they need a new high. Sometimes this manifested in their sexual desires.

Some women loved this. I had a girlfriend, Lana, from the adult film industry who was a total sex addict. She just couldn't get enough and always tried to reach a higher level of sex. This wasn't me. Despite all my acting in movies, at heart, I'm a simple girl who likes normal sex. I like romance and making love.

Lana, however, was a flat-out pervert. I once went to a video store with her where she gave the clerk a code word. In exchange, he handed her a brown paper bag with a video in it. The movie was called *Brown* or something like that, and it was one of the most disgusting films I'd ever seen. People were having sex and then defecating on one another. There was even a scene where a woman hammered a dude's penis to a ladder. I literally got sick. To this day, I believe those actors must have been blackmailed into doing that film.

Lana thought it was great, but Lana was a twisted sex addict who was continuously pushing the limits for shock value. She once took me to an S&M bar with her and her husband. They were swingers, of course, and people were doing the craziest shit in that club. People were tied up and someone even sewed a girl's mouth shut. There was even a liquid they would pour onto people's bodies to set them on fire. I never understood the sexual appeal in pain and torture, but for Lana, it was a total turn-on.

Lana was the one who introduced me to a well-known financial mogul who was one of the most perverted men I've ever met. I was really curious as to what he did for a living, and he said he did something with money exchange in Europe.

The night started off normal enough. He cooked steaks for us on the barbeque and we sat down for dinner. Afterwards, he called someone to bring him about 10 eight balls of methamphetamine. He called it "ice" and said it had been imported straight from Japan. I felt the effect of the drugs almost immediately. I've never felt so alert in my life, as if I could see the lint on a person's sweater.

After dinner, he wanted to watch a movie. He started with just run-of-the-mill porn that eventually progressed into racier movies involving sadomasochism and a leather-clad dominatrix. From there, the films got much grittier. It was nothing like *50 Shades of Gray*. This stuff was dark. I watched in horror as a woman was drawn into a room full of S&M gear, including some kind of guillotine.

At first, I laughed when I saw it. It was so ridiculous that I thought it had to be phony. After a couple minutes, I realized it was real. It couldn't get worse, could it? Yes, it could. The next scene was a guy in a flannel shirt driving along a country road in a pickup. Everything was covered in snow with the tree branches frozen under a film of hoarfrost. The tires crunched the snow in what was almost an idyllic silence until the man stopped and got out into a thicket of bushes. He broke trail by punching through the limbs until he got to a bucket overturned on the ground.

Under the frozen bucket was a young girl buried up to her neck in the frozen ground. The man violently face fucked her, leaving semen and piss in her mouth before covering her head again. I have never seen anything so dark in my life and I was stricken with fear over who this man was and how he could sit there watching this with a faint smile on his face.

I tried to keep my cool, but I was terrified he was going to whip out a knife and start doing the same thing to me, and that my mangled body would be discovered in some dumpster somewhere. I was supposed to spend the night and leave in the morning, but I'd had enough. I told him it was getting really dark. The tipping point for me was when he put peanut butter on his penis and made his dog lick it off. It traumatized me. It was the first time I'd ever been near anyone so sick and twisted.

On another job, I was sent to meet a rich, white guy. He drove a Bentley. When I got to his house, he was sitting on the couch with a tray of cocaine on his lap. The pile was enormous, and he stuck his face right into the middle of it.

This was my first time being around anyone who was so hardcore with drugs. Some of the clients would specifically request girls that would party. Normally, I stuck with alcohol and pills, but this was next level.

I later learned that the guy had been up for days and was completely delirious. Years down the road, he would turn up dead in a seedy hotel. The drugs got the best of him and he lost everything. It was really sad to see someone so wealthy and successful hit rock bottom.

Another night, I went to the home of a man who turned out to be a major crackhead. He smoked these big gumballs of crack, so much so that both his dogs had asthma and would sit there wheezing as they tried to breathe.

My years with Madame Naomi were much tamer. The

madame was actually my friend, and she answered the phone in this insanely high-pitched girly voice. The girls were all former adult film actresses and the clients were mostly our fans. When the porn industry toppled with the advent of high-speed Internet, many of us turned to escorting to pay the bills.

I never felt unsafe in these situations. The men were diehard fans, and we girls definitely had the upper hand. The men thought of us as goddesses, and Madame Naomi was always on hand to make sure nothing happened. Plus, the girls knew how to take care of themselves.

I did get robbed on a job with another one of my friends, though. Men in masks barrelled into our hotel room, tied us up, and robbed us at gunpoint. My girlfriend managed to untie her hands and run downstairs to tell the desk clerk to call the police. The hotel just so happened to get footage of the men leaving, and soon the police were chasing them down Sunset Boulevard after they dumped the gun at a famous hotel called the Mondrian.

They got arrested, and it turned out that we had been set up by someone I had considered a friend. He was the son of a famous soul singer, and his uncle had been the getaway driver.

I had to go to court to testify against the men. During cross-examination, the man's lawyer brought out a photograph of me sitting in a swing with S&M gear on. It was from a shoot I did in a film. The lawyer asked if it was true that I was into

S&M. I replied that I wasn't into people tying me up and stealing my money.

I hadn't even wanted to testify in the first place after I found out that I knew the guys who did it. I told the attorney that my memory was blurred and I couldn't remember exactly what had happened. The creepiest part of the whole experience was that I had just been with the guy and one of his friends at a Hollywood mansion earlier in the week and had no idea they were planning to rob us because they knew we had large sums of money on us. This was before the days of cash apps; back then, it was cash.

Though I escaped those years without physical harm, sex with all these strange and sometimes incredibly depraved men started to really impact my psyche. I felt like I was becoming one of them: a sexual deviant. The drugs, too, really started to impact my life. My personal and work lives were starting to collide, and I needed to find a way to separate the two.

I went to see a therapist who told me to imagine I was two people: one, Dominique, the sex goddess film actress and escort; the other, Deidre, a mom who preferred blue jeans and T-shirts and staying home with her kids. She said to metaphorically think of myself as wearing two different outfits for Domonique and Deidre. When I got home, I was to unzip Dominique and put on Deidre. I told her, "Man, that's an awful lot of zipping on and off."

It worked to a point, but it didn't stop the forces I couldn't control, namely evil spirits that attached themselves to me as a result of the men I slept with. I read somewhere that a person's aura sticks with you for 14 days after you've had sex. Multiply that by all the men I had been with, and that's a lot of evil juju hanging around.

It seemed to be everywhere. Even just walking in downtown Hollywood, you see a lot of people who are spiritually touched. And being in the sex industry, you are more prone to things attaching to you because you're coming into contact with so many different types of people, many of whom are lost souls as they pass you. It's like the world stands still, and it's just that person slowly moving toward you. When you stare at their face, you wonder what kind of sick and vile – and potentially dangerous – things they might be thinking. It takes a toll on the way you see the world.

Some of the shots I did for films and photographs enhanced this sense of evil and danger lurking under the surface. One time, I did a shot at Joshua Tree, a place that is known to be enchanted, with a well-known photographer and filmmaker. In my mind, the place was anything but enchanted. When I think of magical places, I envision birds and butterflies and deer running across pathways full of bunnies. This place by contrast was dark and looming with crooked trees and menacing, sheer rock faces.

The shot in question required me to go under the murky water in a small lake and emerge as if newly baptized. I don't know how to swim and never liked water, so when I went under, something began to pull me down and the photographer had to jump in to save me. It was very creepy and eerie.

After the shot, I went to stay at my friend's house. I went to sleep and suddenly awoke to feel someone touching me. I felt like something was breathing on my vagina and opening my legs, a pressure like someone heavy was lying on top of me. Not a human. Somebody much heavier and larger, like a giant. My friend said he woke up when he heard me making murmuring sounds, and he could see deep impressions of fingerprints on my body. He was horrified and never spoke to me again.

Another experience that traumatized me was posing in a pool with a snake and strawberries and cream. I had to stand in the pool in a bathing suit with a strawberry and whipped cream in my mouth. I have a fear of snakes, and even today, I can't look at that video of me and the snake without cringing.

The snake wrangler took the six-foot-plus snake out of its bag and began wrapping it around my body. I was wearing a cheetah-print bikini and had to lay on the floor, holding the snake's head away from my face. The snake ended up slithering out of my hand and snuggling between my boobs. The wrangler said the snake liked the feel and the sound of my heartbeat. That was one of the most horrifying days for me. When a snake is wrapped around your body, you can feel every muscle in its body moving. It's the creepiest feeling, and one that sticks with me to this day.

All of these events seemed to portend evil forces at work.

It got to the point where the poltergeists began impacting my home. I felt like I was living with demons. My oldest son began seeing things. He claimed he saw doors slam shut, and one night he said he walked into my room and I was screaming; he said it looked like someone was choking me, and he, too, started wailing.

I reached out to my friend Brian, who introduced me to Barry Taff. Taff is a world-renowned parapsychologist who had investigated thousands of cases of ghosts, hauntings, and poltergeists and was well-known and respected for his work in the field. Brian is the son of Doris Bither, who contacted Taff after she alleged that the ghosts of three men were raping her at her home in Culver City in the early '70s. Her case inspired Frank De Felitta's book, *The Entity*, which was made into a 1982 film starring Barbara Hershey.

I spoke to Taff over the phone. On our first call, he told me I was wearing a white T-shirt. He was right. He then told me he realized he had a gift when he was in high school. One of his teachers had a colonoscopy bag that he wore hidden beneath his clothes. Nobody knew he had that bag, except Taff, who questioned why he wore it. The teacher was so shocked he referred Taff to the principal who then called his parents to explain that their son had a mental problem.

Taff had tapped into the spirit world, and I recognized

he could help me. He said he sensed that there was some kind of psychokinesis activity or poltergeist in my world and suggested I go back and look at all the places where I'd spent significant time or lived. He also said that it was very common for women in my industry to experience such entities, especially since I was a single mom facing challenges with my family. He directed me to a website that verified whether or not someone had died at a particular address and another that provided addresses when you entered your name.

The first address that came up when I searched my name was 10050 Cielo Drive in Benedict Canyon. I was surprised to see this because I had never lived there. In fact, the home belonged to Jeff Franklin, the creator of *Full House*, whom I had been dating for the past year.

I'd always found it strange when I pulled into Jeff's long, windy driveway that there was typically a group of people staring at the house from the other side of the fence. Back then, it hadn't struck me as odd, because I just thought they were star-struck fans hoping to get a photo of Jeff. However, when I asked Jeff about the crowd, he said that something very bad had happened in the home years ago, but he never told me what it was.

Something bad was right. It turned out the house formerly belonged to Sharon Tate. It was the very house where Charles Manson's followers murdered her and four others in August 1969. After watching a documentary on the murders, I realized that Jeff's bedroom also belonged to Sharon, so I was sleeping in the same room where she had been murdered. Jeff had done some updates on the upstairs room but left the bedroom completely intact. His bed was even in the same place as hers, near the sliding glass door. The same hot tub where her body had been found was also still in the bedroom. It was completely creepy, and I was stunned he hadn't told me about it.

(Oddly enough, Jeff's maid worked for Richard Pryor and was the person who found him after he set himself on fire in 1980. He had poured rum on his shirt and set himself ablaze while freebasing cocaine.)

I was stunned that Jeff never told me this was the Tate mansion. We dated off and on for about a year, but I stopped seeing him shortly after finding this out, and it still freaks me out that I was sleeping in the same room where those murders occurred.

I also learned there had been a killing in my apartment building. A young girl had been kidnapped from one of the units, and the police shut the place down as they searched for her. They ended up finding the girl dead and stuffed in a closet. The killer was a college student and the girl's father's neighbor. He'd kidnapped, raped, and killed her. His hands were so tight around her mouth during the assault that he left palm imprints. He ended up slitting his wrists and killing himself, too, when he realized there was no way to escape the building.

I lived in this apartment complex on three different occasions following the murder. I was never able to find out what unit the murder occurred in because the police wouldn't release those details.

Given my life at the time, it made sense that I would be ripe grounds for bad spirits. I think of Brian's mom, Doris, who had been a troubled mom raising three kids, similar to myself, when the poltergeists began raping her. She wasn't physically or emotionally healthy, and I think this weakens your defenses against evil spirits. Who is to say that something evil, either in the Tate house or elsewhere, hadn't attached itself to me?

Convinced I was inflicted, I went to see a Catholic priest to help exorcize the evil spirits. When I walked in, it was a sunny afternoon and lights were streaming through the big stained-glass windows. Shards of gold lit a nativity scene where adoring shepherds grasped their hearts as they smiled down on baby Jesus. I felt a holy presence that emboldened me to seek help.

I went into an office where a receptionist sat behind a heavy oak desk. There was something solid about it that made me feel comfortable. I told her that I was experiencing some issues in my home. It was spiritual warfare, I explained, asking what steps needed to be taken. She told me there was a priest who worked with people in my position. She made an appointment for me to see him.

When I came back, the priest led me into a dark, musty

room to the side of the altar. He was wearing all black like he was preparing to perform an exorcism. I felt cold as he began praying over me.

He asked me if I needed a coat, then took off his jacket and gave it to me to put on. I put my head down as he prayed over me. There were others helping him in the room, and it went on for at least a few hours. Eventually, someone helped me up and assisted me to the door. I walked on rubbery legs, totally out of it, back to my car and home. When I walked in, my cat made a beeline out of the room.

I never felt so exhausted in all my life. As if that experience wasn't taxing and strange enough, that night, a friend called and asked me if they could bring a young lady to my house. Apparently, she had overdosed and was recently released from the ER. The funny thing was that I almost didn't answer the phone when I saw whose number was on the caller ID. This was a person I had sworn that I would never speak to again, but when I saw his name, I couldn't bring myself to not answer. He knew that in the past, I had often taken in people who were experiencing problems with their boyfriends or marriages or who were otherwise in need. I told him, yes, he could drop the woman off and I would take care of her.

When the young lady walked into my home, I saw death. She was a walking skeleton. I led her to the couch and gave her a warm blanket. Throughout the night, I could hear her making these grunting sounds, which scared me. I remembered that I had a crucifix in my house, so I took it and I put it in her hands while she was sleeping.

The next day, I woke up with the sun shining into my bedroom and beaming on my face. I could hear a voice in the next room, saying "What the fuck is happening?" The woman's drugs had worn off and she had no idea where she was, so I explained that my friend had dropped her off the night before. She sat up and seemed completely normal and not at all fazed that she'd just woken up at a stranger's home with a crucifix in her hand. Gone was the woman who had arrived last night in a drug-induced stupor.

I ended up taking her home later that day. When we got there, it was full of people who had been living there for several months, just mooching off her and not paying any rent. I was really shocked because it was such a nice house, and from the outside, you wouldn't expect a flop house.

It was as if she'd completely given up on getting rid of these people. She told me she wanted to get some things before they stole everything. She said these people had given her some ecstasy the night prior and essentially left her there to die. It was clear she needed help, so I invited her to stay at my home. After my experience at the Catholic church, I believed that God had put us into each other's paths.

She went into her bedroom and began pulling clothes out of her closet. At the time, I had a huge Hummer, and she just started throwing stuff into the back of my truck:

Christian Dior blouses, Louis Vuitton bags, everything was designer. She loaded up her arms with as much as she could carry and let the guests know she was leaving. They wanted to know whether or not she'd be taking her dog. It was the saddest thing. We went into the backyard, where her dog was chained up with its water and food dish out of reach. It yanked on its chain to try to get to the food and water. I've never been a dog person, but there was no way that I was letting her leave the dog there with those people.

Later that night, she told me all about herself, and she had a wild story. Her father had once managed Elvis; she actually gave me a shirt that Elvis had worn in one of his movies. She had a lot of memorabilia, including the death certificate of Marilyn Monroe, whom her father also managed. The certificate said Marilyn died from a barbiturate overdose, and it appeared to be real.

She had a bunch of things she inherited from her dad when he passed away that she brought to my house. She talked about going to a treatment center and asked if she could leave her belongings at my home.

The next day, I woke up to music blaring. When I went into the room where she was staying, she was hovered in a corner wearing ripped stockings with black eyeliner smudged around her eyes. She looked like a demented Amy Winehouse; an entirely different person than the woman I'd just spent the past day with. Her dad's memorabilia was scattered in piles around her. Apparently, she'd rifled through everything, looking for drugs until she found some. She had relapsed and transformed into a whole new person.

It was the scariest thing I'd ever seen. She ended up doing her makeup and getting dressed in a skirt with a very slutty garter belt. I told her she couldn't leave my house dressed like the fucking Joker. I asked her what she was thinking, and she said she looked good. She ended up leaving my house that night and I never saw her again.

I called the person who had dropped her off at my house in the first place, and they put me in contact with someone who knew her. It turned out that someone had found her behind an IHOP doing some type of fashion show in her lingerie. Apparently, she was walking back and forth as if on a runway until someone called the police and she was committed to a mental hospital. Eventually, someone who knew her came to my house to collect her belongings to put in storage, but I always had a weird feeling, as if those items she brought into my home had a spiritual connection to something darker. After that, my house never felt the same.

Evil spirits aside, I continued to see a therapist, Dr. Faye Snyder, to help work through some of the residual issues that had been impacting me for decades.

Dr. Faye was familiar with evil and darkness. She'd spent 16 hours with the serial killer Richard Ramirez, who had raped and tortured at least 14 people in the summer of 1985, while he was on death row. She asked him if he'd ever spared any of his victims. Surprisingly, the answer was yes.

Ramirez told Dr. Faye that one night, he picked a house and climbed in through the window. He heard the sounds of a TV and walked down the hall to the den, where he found a woman watching a show. She looked up and said to him, "Oh my God! Who did this to you?" Ramirez told Dr. Faye that he sat down and talked to this woman for 20 minutes. He told her about his life, his relationship with his mother, and all the abuse he had endured over time. Then he got up and left.

I felt so grateful to be alive after all the precarious chances I'd taken with my life, and I knew it was time to finally leave the sex industry. I needed to rid my world of all this darkness. I wanted something better for both myself and my children. It wasn't about just making money: I wanted a purpose and opportunity to do good with my life.

Little did I realize that just because I was ready to move on, it didn't mean my past would remain hidden. No matter what I did with my future, there was no way to get rid of Domonique Simone.

Dancing with the Devil

10

FALLEN ANGELS

The porn industry is not easy on people. There are a lot of casualties, and many actresses and actors do not live long. I read somewhere that the average lifespan for a porn star is 26; many die at the peak of their careers. It's an industry rife with drug overdoses, mental health issues, suicide, and sometimes murder. Several of my close friends from the industry were among these casualties.

Off the top of my head, I can name more than a dozen that I personally knew, including Buck Adams Jamoo, Cal Jammer, Woody Long, Savannah, Tricia, Kyle Stone, Lai Lonni, Anna Amore, Anna Malle, Julie Strain, and John Dough. I worked with all of them.

These deaths primarily involved car accidents, overdoses, HIV, suicides, or murders. Most recently, Alicia Rio died from complications of COVID-19.

A rash of deaths between December 2017 and January 2018 dominated the headlines when five female porn stars between the ages of 20 and 35 died within two months.

Many publications ran articles asking why adult film stars were suffering and dying.

It can be a tough world. Almost everyone I knew had drug and alcohol problems on top of mental health issues that were sometimes exacerbated by an industry that's heavily looked down upon by the outside world. Many girls came to Hollywood looking for their big break, and some got exploited by greedy, unethical movie producers.

Then there's the issue of our love lives, which could be disastrous. One of my friends ended up meeting and marrying a guy she met in the psych ward who took her home, tied her up, and stuck pins in her before stealing her car. I asked her what the hell she was thinking, marrying someone she met in a psych ward.

Drugs are also a big problem, and some women, like Lacey, died before they could kick the habit. I met Lacey when she was 18. She looked a lot like Jennifer Lopez, and she wanted me to take her under my wing and help her get into the industry. She'd been working as an escort but wanted to leave the world to become an actress.

She landed an audition to be on *The Real World* but ended up missing it because she was hanging out doing drugs. She was really upset about it because she wanted the chance to do something legit with her life. The two of us stayed in touch for a few years until she died of a drug overdose. She never did make it out.

I also had a pretty serious drug problem. I was even

rumored to have died of a drug overdose in Atlanta. According to one website, I died twice. My drug use never impacted my ability to work, unlike for other stars who let their addiction derail their lives and showed up high or drunk on set. I never did that when I was working.

My drug use, however, got much worse after I left the industry and started working as an escort. My addiction almost brought me down and put me in some precarious situations. Looking back, it's hard to admit that to anyone, including myself.

For a time, it was pretty bad. It started off with ecstasy and cocaine. Then I chased the dragon, smoking heroin. I remember the first night I did it and how sick I felt the next day. I'd gone to an industry party with my neighbor, who worked for MTV. Girls were smoking in a corner and I joined them. I had no idea what it was, but I called my neighbor the next day to tell her I felt really sick. She explained it was the "H." I had no idea, but then I was hooked.

I'm ashamed to say that sometimes, when my neighbor and I couldn't find drugs, I would drive down to a shady park in LA, where people went to score. It was a horribly scary experience, so we would take turns. We'd pull up to the park and men would pop up from behind bushes with balloons in their mouths (they put them in there so they could swallow the drugs if cops tried to bust them).

Once, I went by myself to San Francisco so I could go on a bender in a city where nobody knew me. I dressed up in a little schoolgirl skirt and little white tank with $20,000 stuffed in my purse. I went to the Tenderloin district, where people literally sell their tender little asses to get drugs. Because I didn't know anyone, I asked a stranger where to get drugs. I gave him a wad of cash and asked him to bring the drugs back to my room, the presidential suite at the Ritz Carlton.

I was shocked when he and his girlfriend showed up to my suite with the drugs. He said it had always been their dream to spend one night in this hotel. I let them spend the night there and was so touched by his honesty and niceness that I ended up putting them up in the room for a month. I was worried about them being okay and didn't think twice about myself.

Eventually, I was able to get clean, but it took decades.

The scariest thing that ever happened to me occurred early in my career when I was just getting started in adult films. Later, I would find out that I almost starred in my own personal snuff film. It was one of the most frightening things that ever happened to me in my life, and even today, I still feel sick to my stomach just thinking about it.

I was 18 and had just dropped out of school after doing my first magazine shoot and first scene in an adult film. Making that kind of money left me naively open to other opportunities to make bank by showing my flesh. I was also very broke, and my roommate and I were about to be evicted from our apartment.

I was walking home from an audition that afternoon. I wasn't really paying attention to where I was going, and I ended up on a seedy street in Hollywood known to be frequented by prostitutes and drug addicts. It was the middle of the day, so I felt relatively safe. That's when two Middle Eastern men pulled up beside me in a white van.

Looking back, that van should have set off all kinds of alarms. Today, in the age of human trafficking and the prevalence of missing person cases, I see it clearly as the stereotypical "creeper van." Back then, however, I was a young girl who had just made lots of money doing a film shoot and my first scene in an adult film. I figured this would be an easy way to make $500.

As soon as I got into the back of the van, the hairs on my neck stood up. I held my breath and frantically craned my neck to see through the windshield where we were going. The van was dirty and smelled like the bottom of a dumpster. All I could smell was the putrid, sour odor of rotting trash. There were no windows in the back of the van and it was eerily silent and dark.

The men drove and seemed to be arguing in Arabic as one gestured to pull the van over. We parked along a desolate street in a part of LA that I didn't recognize. Suddenly, one of the guys grabbed a camera and aggressively pulled me out of my seat into the back of the van. I didn't even have time to process what was happening.

I told the guys I wanted to leave, and one of them handed

me $50 and told me to shut the hell up. The other guy kept turning around to look through the front window to see if anyone was coming. When I turned my head, I really saw a roll of tape, a pile of zip ties, and what looked like a big pair of tree clippers.

I started to scream. The man closest to me covered my mouth and tried to tape it shut. I bit him, and he pulled out a gun. He then grabbed me by the throat and put the cocked gun to my head. He forcibly grabbed my breasts and yanked my head back so abruptly it felt as if it had snapped.

The look of excitement in their eyes added to my terror as a jolt of electricity zapped through my body. It was beyond terrifying because they seemed so comfortable in their actions. I couldn't help but wonder how many other women they'd had in the van and how many managed to walk out alive.

They started talking to each other. One of the guys said they had to kill me because I'd seen their faces. He held me down while the other guy tried to tie up my feet. I screamed louder, and with all my strength, I managed to kick open the back door. The guys panicked and pushed me out of the van.

I ran toward a parking lot and saw it was a Jack in the Box fast food restaurant. I ran inside and waited for hours, watching for the van. They circled around the building a couple of times, so I stayed still in the restaurant until I thought the coast was clear.

When it started to get dark, I figured it was time to make a getaway. I ran home through backyards, jumping fences. I've never been so scared in my life. It was like something out of a horror film. I was literally running for my life.

I recently saw a YouTube video about guys who were picking up girls and raping and killing them. I could have very much been one of those girls. I had no family in town and only knew a few people. I was totally vulnerable. It would have been so easy for them to kill me and dump the body. Nobody had cell phones or cameras back then. It would have been easy for them to get away with it.

I still have flashbacks of myself running through traffic and backyards to get away from those men. It never goes away. The most chilling aspect is knowing that someone else had control of my life and the power to snuff it out.

The sad thing is, some people would say I deserved to die. That's what comes with working in the sex industry. In many people's eyes, we're disposable and get what we deserve, especially if we are choosing to sell our bodies for sex. For most of us in the industry, it's just a business. Like everyone else, we're trying to make a living, and there's a great deal of stress that comes with maintaining stardom in an image-based industry.

The amount of work it takes to stay at the top of your game and constantly redefine your image to stay relevant cannot be overstated. There are always dozens of girls behind you who are vying for your position, trying to dethrone you while you're struggling to stay on top. It's the nature of the beast in an industry where people view you as a doll or toy. You're a physical body, not a person.

Of all my friends who died, I think Savannah's death hit me the hardest. Savannah, whose real name was Shannon Wilsey, left an impression on me. She was a force, and I don't think I'd ever met such a naturally beautiful woman. She looked just like the girl in *Poltergeist,* with white blonde hair and bangs. She didn't even need makeup to be stunning.

I met Savannah at an adult film award show in Vegas. We'd both starred in films with the Italian film star Rocco Siffredi. At the show, I'd gotten up on stage at a nightclub and did a rap song with the owners of Moonlight Video, who had a rock band. Afterwards, I ran into Savannah in the bathroom, and in her sweet little voice, she told me she liked the song. We immediately became friends.

Despite her beauty, it was clear she was broken. It was rumored that she'd experienced abuse at a young age and that she began dating a famous rockstar in high school and later went on the road with him.

Sexual abuse seemed to be a predominant experience for many of us. This abuse, I believe, tends to drive many women like myself into the industry. I often ask myself, had I not been sexually abused as a young girl, would I have so easily fallen into this profession?

There is a type of guy who preys on a young woman's vulnerability. I saw this in a fashion designer who was arrested on charges of sex trafficking and exploiting young women. I met Peter in the early '90s. One of my girlfriends was staying at his beach house in Santa Monica and invited me to a party.

He looked as if he'd stepped right out of a bad plastic surgery ad. He was well-known for having sex parties and would even offer free drugs. Not a lot of guys there were there that night, but the rooms were teeming with young women.

This was not my scene at all and not the type of party I was used to attending. The house was beautiful, as were the young women who were straddling Peter's lap and splayed around the rooms like window dressings. There must have been at least 20 girls in the house and not one of them was over 30. I was 20 at the time, and not into being in this creeper's company. Apparently, he promised these women modeling careers in exchange for sex.

The girls treated him as if he were a god. I was told he had a woman helping him recruit the girls, much like Jeffrey Epstein had. I was disgusted to see my friend engage in a three-way with him and another girl that night. I couldn't figure out why she was staying there, and I asked her what she got out of it. She said he gave her a place to live, and sometimes, money to buy clothes. She wanted to know if I was interested and I said hell no. I was an actress. I had an agent and was in demand. I didn't have to impress anyone. I'd never seen girls act so desperate and I found it humiliating.

I couldn't believe what was going on there and was so glad the authorities finally caught him. A lot of that child trafficking was going on, I just wasn't aware of it.

Savannah had the kind of vulnerability that made her easy prey for men. She was one of the most prominent stars in the industry and skyrocketed to the top in her four-year career in the early '90s. From the first time I met her, she inspired me. I even ended up buying a Corvette because she had one. I just really liked her vibe. She was also a true diva, and I desperately wanted to reach that same level of celebrity. Getting to know her was a huge honor for me, because I learned to be self-confident and step in like a boss. I even started wearing my hair like hers. To me, she embodied everything that was stardom, and I wanted to have what she had.

She was the Jenna Jameson of our time, the "it girl" who crossed over into mainstream films and even walked down the runway for a famous designer. I don't think any other adult film star ever reached her level of fame, with the exception of Traci Lords.

I eventually got there, and some people referred to me as the "Black Savannah." We both had a bunch of haters who talked shit about us and experienced a lot of pressure as superstars from younger women vying to take our place. It was exhausting, but it was nice to have someone else on our side who understood the pressure of maintaining our level of stardom.

Unfortunately, Savannah had a serious drug problem and was chronically in debt. It seemed like no matter how much money she had or how many films she did, it was never enough. She was also notorious for telling people she was planning to kill herself. Because she made so many false claims about suicide, people stopped taking her seriously. She was like the boy who cried wolf, until she eventually did shoot herself. She was the last person I ever thought would take their own life because she had everything going for her, despite the fact that in recent years she had kind of fallen into a slump.

She killed herself in 1994. She'd just moved up to Beverly Hills and was coming through Cold Water Canyon with someone else in the car with her. She hit a pole with her Corvette and broke her nose. After the accident, she went home and took a bath. She saw how bad her nose looked and then shot herself in the head. She'd gotten the gun for protection because someone was stalking her. She died at the hospital.

It's not clear what drove her to do it, but I speculate there were several factors, from her long-term abuse to her recent relationship with the guitarist from a popular rock band (they had made promises to each other, but he would never marry her because she was a porn star).

She also had a relationship with the comedian Pauly Shore, whom I sat next to at her closed-casket funeral. He wasn't embarrassed of her and even took her as his date to the American Music Awards. She was in love with the rockstar, who ended up going to Hawaii and getting married to someone else. He'd married this other woman because she told him she was pregnant with his child. It broke Savannah's heart.

I took the news of her death hard. I was in total shock and truly devastated. I was 23 at the time and she was 22. I was interviewed by Barry Barryson, who was doing a story on her and other stars who tragically died young. He wanted to hear about Savannah from a friend, and also about the adult film industry.

I must have talked to him for seven hours. Up until that point, I thought my lifestyle was normal because it was my world. Talking to him made me see it in a new light. These stories were tragic, and he was really drawn to my story, which gave me pause. Surely, I was not part of this dark world where celebrities die young, tragic, pointless deaths.

He said he wanted to write my book, which planted the idea in my head all those years ago. I wanted a different ending.

This was about the time I realized I wanted to leave the industry. The pressure of maintaining my level of stardom and remaining on top began to feel like a hopeless venture. I wanted to go out on my own terms, not be a pathetic figure trying in vain to hold on to what I once had.

It was time to reinvent myself and create a different future for myself and my kids, far away from the sex industry, where appearance wasn't one's ultimate saving grace. I needed more.

I made a lot of money doing films. I was lucky that I didn't get ripped off by greedy producers wanting to gouge my contracts. Unlike a lot of girls in the industry, I was protected because I had people looking out for me from the very start of my career, watching my back. It was really a matter of timing and luck, and I felt like my fellow stars were like family.

I also worked with great film producers who paid me well and didn't take advantage of me. I never felt alienated within the industry, though I did definitely suffer from my share of mental health issues and drug and alcohol abuse. I also got caught up in doing everything possible to preserve my image and stay on top.

We all knew this when we willingly entered the business, but it takes a toll on a person. There was always the need to modify our bodies with breast enlargements, tummy tucks, and other alterations in order to remain looking good. In many cases, this led stars to undergo constant – and sometimes dangerous – plastic surgeries as well as take drugs to stay thin.

I personally underwent many surgeries trying to look good and stay relevant, from breast enlargements and having my nose done twice to basically starving myself and trying every crash diet; when all that failed, I turned to lipo.

All in all, the pressures of maintaining the perfect body,

coupled with the implied shame of the occupation, was often a lethal recipe for disaster that resulted in many girls dying alone on hospital gurneys in foreign countries. Many girls relied on drugs to maintain their bodies, resulting in a roller coaster of drugs and alcohol – a destructive lifestyle.

These girls were once children with no fears. Some were protected by the world and others emerged from broken families. All were forced to experience the darker side of the world, where they were exposed to the true evilness of people. They started out their lives as angels, and in the end, were fallen.

11

DEATH OF AN INDUSTRY

If I could point to the end of the porn industry as I knew it, it was the introduction of commercial broadband in the late 1990s. Almost overnight, the whole industry imploded. Leading up to that, though, there were other scares, such as the HIV outbreak which started to change the face of the adult film scene and would ultimately drive the industry out of town.

During my day, the San Fernando Valley was porn central. All the A-list actors and movie studios were here, and it was a giant hub for those wanting to get into the business. It looks much different today. We couldn't have predicted the impact of the Internet or the disease that would bring the industry to its knees.

When AIDS was first diagnosed in the 1980s, it was thought to be a virus in the sperm but was later found to be carried in the blood. This is why it was prevalent among guys who had aggressive anal sex. I can still remember the fear surrounding the virus, which then was considered a death sentence.

The things you have to worry about are typically those you know nothing about. That was true in the case of AIDS. If someone had an STD, it was pretty easy to detect. With AIDS there wasn't a visible tell, so you had no idea if you were infected. There were a lot of women who were likely exposed but didn't know.

Keep in mind that up until that point, the industry was pretty loose when it came to having unprotected sex. In my day, we didn't use condoms and instead relied on Today sponges, which ended up being really dangerous for women and aren't around anymore. Not until HIV came along did people start really taking precautions seriously.

We had to do regular STD panels and take HIV PCR tests at least once a month. The worst part was sitting there waiting for the results. If a person got called back in, you knew they had it. A positive diagnosis cost a person their film career, and in many cases, their lives.

I got lucky, but others were not as fortunate. One male film star changed his test results and lied about having the virus. He ended up infecting about 20 people in the industry, including one prominent African American female star. It wasn't her fault, but it did impact her career, and she was forced to leave the industry.

There were other scares. A female porn star from Europe tested positive and infected 10 other people. Another group of actors was infected after doing a film with a transsexual in Brazil.

It was a really scary time for all of us. I had just done an orgy scene for a huge film they were reshooting. There were about 30 girls and 20 guys on set and seven actors ended up getting exposed. The outbreak caused mass hysteria, forcing the business to temporarily shut down while doctors came on set to do seminars about the dangers.

The crisis hit a tipping point in the early 1990s when a guy went on the news to say that his porn star girlfriend was HIV positive. It wasn't true, but sounding the alarm caught the attention of the public health department. They shut down the industry for two to three months, after which we were all required to take classes to learn about the disease and how we could avoid getting infected.

That's when porn legend Sharon Mitchell started the AIM Foundation for testing. I have so much respect for Sharon for starting the clinic. Prior to that, we had to go to a testing center in Venice, California that was owned by a plastic surgeon. At the new center, we'd get our test results in five minutes.

It was pretty much the scariest five minutes of your life, waiting to get those test results. They would call us back to do the blood draw and then put the vial of blood in this spinning machine. It felt like a lifetime of waiting; a potential death sentence, as if you were playing Russian roulette.

Then they would call you back to give you your results.

They did this for confidentiality reasons, but speculation was there regardless. It's completely horrifying to think that we had to do this once a month, then once a week, then every time we shot a movie.

The doors of the clinic were closed in 2011 due to a breach where 12,000 adult performers' information was released publicly.

I know of several people who tested positive. One person ended up getting $250,000 from the Social Security Administration for contracting the virus on a movie set. That was the first time that's ever been done in the history of porn. The star in question was a dear friend of mine who contracted the virus while doing a 100-guy gangbang.

It was a pivotal moment in the adult film industry. The state health department got involved and began cracking down. When California passed a law requiring adult film stars to wear condoms, producers began looking elsewhere, to Europe or to states with more lenient rules.

The production company I worked for sent me to Europe to make some films in Italy. I was cast with one of the biggest Italian stars at the time, Rocco Siffredi, who was known as the "Italian Stallion," for good reason. I can safely say he was one of the hottest guys in the industry.

We did three films together. I met Rocco when he was brought in to work with Taylor Wayne on her birthday. I was sleeping in the studio at the time. Sometimes we would wait for 12 hours between scenes, so many of us would nap on the couches. I remember waking up to a beautiful man standing in front of me putting on an Armani suit.

He looked up when he saw me and lamented in a heavy Italian accent that he'd just gotten circumcised and that they'd cut off two inches of his dick. I was the first African American girl that he ever slept with. The scene involved three other girls, but I quickly dominated him. We had serious chemistry, and the director could see we really clicked.

Europe, in general, was so much more progressive when it came to pornography. They didn't want to see condoms and were much more open about sexuality in general. When I was in France for the Cannes Adult Film Festival, porn played on television during the day. Women walked around topless on the beaches. They don't have the same puritanical hang-ups about sex that we have here in the States.

I really enjoyed my time in France and Italy. I brought my then-boyfriend – a model – with me to France. We made the front page of the newspaper when he flipped off the paparazzi. The headline was "American hospitality" with a big picture of the two of us staring down the cameras as he flipped them the bird.

Apart from the relentless press, it was one of the best trips of my life. We stayed at a small inn in the countryside that felt like someone's home. I remember sitting on the terrace while my boyfriend strummed his guitar barefoot. It was idyllic and so peaceful, one of those moments that remains vivid in my mind.

I also understood how lucky I was to be an American adult film star. On the set, the director wanted me to do anal, but I explained that it was not in my contract, so the director brought in a handful of beautiful Hungarian girls to do the anal shots. They had taken the train over from Hungary and were only being paid $300 for the day. The girls were desperate and needed the money to buy food for their families. The director took advantage of their vulnerability. In my life, I've never seen girls handled so roughly. They did at least four anal scenes I'd never seen before, with their bodies horribly twisted.

It looked so painful that my boyfriend actually started crying because he thought that that was how I was being treated. It wasn't. The producers abided by the terms of my contract and paid me $10,000 a day. I felt terrible for those girls.

I never got used to watching myself in these foreign films. I'd see a Black woman with triple-D boobs speaking French and it took me a while to realize I was watching myself, the dubbing was so perfect.

The industry in the U.S. was rocked by controversy when two underage girls – Traci Lords and Alexandria Quinn– were busted. Quinn was 17 when she did her first film while Lords was only 15. Both had used fake IDs, and when it was discovered that they'd lied, many of their films were pulled from circulation and either scrapped or re-edited. I don't think it happened that often, but some girls definitely broke the law.

After that, film execs really cracked down. They made you show two forms of ID and recorded you answering questions about the nature of the roles you would be playing. This was in response to one adult film star who claimed she had been raped because she had been throat fucked to the point where she vomited. To prevent this from happening again, the producer would ask you to state exactly what you would be expected to do sexually in that film.

But the advent of the Internet would ultimately produce the biggest blow to the industry. Almost overnight, porn as we knew it was wiped out when dial-up Internet was introduced. Suddenly, all of the content – most of which was pirated – was available online in the comfort of people's homes.

Prior to dial-up, porn DVDs sold for $150. A few years later, those same videos were being rented out at video stores for $5. If that wasn't bad enough, fiber optics and live streaming came along not long after and caused even more destruction.

We soon went from making $10,000 to $5,000 a day. The billion-dollar porn industry was upended, with producers and actors no longer making the lion's share of the profit. Social media and other apps further watered down the need for adult films, as amateurs shared pics, videos, and stolen content for free. We didn't get any residuals for our films.

No longer did guys need to go to strip clubs or movie theaters, because they could watch porn on their computers from the comfort – and anonymity – of their homes. This is when the business got darker.

The industry today is nothing like it was back when I was working. The 1990s in general were just a magical time for adult films. We were consummate professionals who took our scripts and acting seriously. The storylines were a big part of the films, and many of us did cross-over and mainstream soft porn for late-night cable channels. Today, there's nothing in the films to even suggest a story. It's just one sex scene after another, and it seems to only get more aggressive, from cream pies and ass to mouth to double anal and 100-guy gang bangs.

Think about it: 100-guy gang bangs. My friend actually did this, and she contracted AIDS as a result. The most I ever did was seven guys, which by today's standards would be considered softcore porn. As Howard Stern told me when I went on his show, that's hardly even a gangbang. The record was 500 guys at one time. Granted, it took that one a couple of weeks to film rather than one session as portrayed in the movie. That actress' career skyrocketed after the film, which I found appalling. Who would want to touch her after all those men? Most people don't even sleep with 500 guys over the course of a lifetime.

It makes me sad to see an industry that I was once involved

with become so violent and crass. All things considered, it felt like the perfect time to get out. I was 27 at that point and a new mother. I liked the idea of leaving at the top of my game and letting people wonder what happened to me. At this point, I had done close to 300 films, was probably the best-known African American porn star, and had one hell of a career. It was time to do something else.

I'm often asked if I'd ever consider doing a film today. The answer is hell no. Not only would I not do that as a mother of four children, but you couldn't pay me enough to be affiliated with an industry that I feel has become far too extreme and dangerous.

I got out at the right time. Many people wonder if I regret having been an adult film star given the negative ramifications it caused in some areas of my life. The answer is still no. I don't. I loved making adult films, and my fellow actors gave me a family when I really needed one. I was a lost girl on my own when I arrived in LA, and the adult film industry allowed me to make a great living and see and experience a world I would have never otherwise been able to access.

I also feel like I paved the way for other Black women in the sex industries. When I started in the field, I wasn't always hired at first. Once, I even walked into an adult video store in the South where they covered all the interracial sex films with bags. Until I worked with big companies such as Video Team, I got passed over on a lot of auditions.

In one instance that I am ashamed to admit, I took a part in a film with Shawn Michaels called *Black Mariah*. Shawn hadn't read the script before filming. After we did our scenes, he got ahold of the script and we were horrified to see how Black people were portrayed in this "spoof." It was supposed to be a cultural spoof but it came out more as racial stereotyping. Not only was there a white guy in Blackface but the film also depicted Black characters eating watermelon. The producer tried to defend himself by saying that they were making fun of all races, but it didn't sit right with us.

In my case, I was cast as an oversexualized Black woman. At the time, I didn't understand the historical ramifications of this typecasting because I had just been following the director's directions for my role. The scenes were filmed on separate days, so we didn't see it until it was released. I felt bad about my role in that film, which came off as racist. I saw no humor in it.

In another case, I signed a contract with a company to do a film called *Black Jack City*. After doing a few scenes, I found out the film was depicting African American women as hookers. I told the director I didn't want to take part in anything that perpetuated negative stereotypes about Black women or any movie that referred to them as "hos." I was told that if I walked out, I'd lose the contract. I left, but the director still put my scenes in the film.

I ran into racism early in my career, particularly on the

dancing side. Some agents didn't want to book me in clubs. In other instances, I ran up against colorism. One Black club owner, for instance, didn't want to book me because he said I was too white and wouldn't attract Black men.

It paid to be lighter, I have to admit. In many instances, my makeup artist would make me lighter because I sold more films if my image was whiter in the cover shot. Critics called me the Michael Jackson of porn and accused me of intentionally whitening my skin, but I never did that cosmetically, only for cover shots. It was different back then. There weren't iPhones and apps that allowed you to easily manipulate photos. Everything had to be done with makeup and cameras.

Overall, though, I think Black film stars had a harder time when it came to discrimination. Some of the white porn stars had clauses in their contracts exempting them from starring with Black men, because films with white women didn't sell as well when they were with Black guys. Producers and film execs went with combinations that sold, primarily Black women and white actors.

Some of the women accused me of not wanting to work with Black men, but that wasn't true. Were it up to me, Lexington Steele would be on the top of my list. He was one of my favorite actors to work with, along with Peter North, Rocco, TT, and Randy Spears.

Another regret is that I didn't save more money or invest in my future. But those are lessons learned. I was glad to leave at the height of my career on my own terms before I became a has-been or burned out. It's an industry for young women; older women have an expiration date unless they take up directing or camera work. I would rather have had people wondering what happened to me and asking if I planned to return.

My last film was *Booty Talk* with Lexington Steele. He was big in the industry, and we dated briefly. He'd talked me into doing the film because the two of us were dating at the time, but that in itself was a disaster. He was a known swinger. I myself have never been much into swinging. There's something about seeing someone I love having sex with another person that just does not sit with me. It's kind of shocking given that I'm in the porn business, but I just don't like it.

But I did go to a swinging party with him. It was the most uncomfortable feeling. We walked in and all these people were having sex in front of us. The strangest part was that they were looking at us as if we were supposed to just take off our clothes and jump in. Men were passing off their wives and girlfriends to other people, and all around us, couples were having sex in booths and makeshift beds set up in rooms and hallways. I felt like I was in a dream sequence and could feel the people undressing me with their eyes. It was the creepiest sensation.

We ended up bringing a girl home with us and engaging in a three-way. My head was spinning and all I could see was red because I was so angry. The combination of passion and bitter outrage was too much for me to bear. I went into the bathroom and left them having sex in Lex's study. Porn videos were blaring on his big screen TVs as I got dressed and slipped out his side door to my car. As I drove off, I could see Lex in my rearview mirror, running after me with his pants in his hands.

Admittedly, he had a hold on me. He even talked me into another sexual encounter with him and his ex-wife. I ran into them the night before Halloween. I was in a store, shopping for a costume for a party, when this girl with an accent walked up to me. She was so polite. She told me that she was Lexington's wife and thought I was really beautiful. I had not seen him since that last night, but she was so sweet and stunningly beautiful. She asked for my phone number, but I never thought she'd contact me.

The next day, however, I had a message from her. She wanted to know if I wanted to hang out with her and Lex. I returned her call and found myself at their home later that evening.

It was strange being there with her. I began to let the feelings that I had for him start to overwhelm me, but at the same time, I had this beautiful woman in front of me who was so sexy; all I could think about was ravishing her. Lex kind of kicked back and gave us our space. We drank and partied while he cowered in the corner, tentatively watching as if he was afraid to even join the party.

We found ourselves watching porn movies, which is the craziest thing you would think that three porn stars would do in a house together. It was a good night.

I have zero resentment toward Lexington because he never tried to lie about who he was. I just wanted more than he could offer.

As for whether I would advise other women to pursue a career in adult films, the answer is more complicated. The industry I was in doesn't exist anymore. It's becoming rougher and grittier as our tolerance for violence and sexual fetishes continues to become more extreme and the dark web becomes more prevalent. The art of well-made porn films with elaborate scripts and professional actors has also gone by the wayside.

I wouldn't want to be an actress in the business right now. I think many girls think that they want to be porn stars because they admire female rap stars and social media influencers who blatantly flaunt their sexuality and make porn seem cool.

Some girls want to get into the industry because they think it will be glamorous or they are looking for a better life. Many come from abusive homes with limited resources and end up being ripped off or exploited. They end up with guys who force them into the industry for their own financial gain. We called these guys "suitcase pimps" because they take girls to hotels and make them work. In some cases, these girls find themselves overdosed or dead.

Some girls come out, but they are not as fortunate to have the resources and career breaks that I did. I got lucky. Part of this was my sheer determination not to go down, but also the blessing of being in the adult film world at the right time and finding good people to guide me. It was not always as glamorous as it seemed and there's definitely a downside to fame.

VICTORIA'S SECRET

12

NEWFOUND MOTHERHOOD

I woke up sick with a snake on the loose. I had been staying with my good friend, June Pointer, in her basement. Her boa constrictor had gotten out of its cage and was slithering somewhere in the basement with me. It was the only thing on my mind as I puked into the toilet. I could barely focus on what I was doing out of fear of being squeezed to death by an oversized reptile. I freaked out anytime I felt something touch my foot.

Despite the distraction, a glooming realization hit me like a thud. Could I be pregnant?

At the time, I was 27, and motherhood couldn't have been further from my mind. I was so busy working and partying that I couldn't imagine taking care of anyone, let alone raising a child. I had just spent the last night at the House of Blues with the Pointer Sisters, where I'd jumped onstage with them and sang backup. June and I were having the time of our lives, and my lifestyle was definitely not conducive to having a baby.

A pregnancy test the next day confirmed my suspicion. I was two months pregnant and strung out on drugs. I didn't have time to contemplate becoming a mother because it was no longer in my hands. My instincts kicked into gear and I immediately checked myself into a one-month, locked-down rehab, leaving behind everything, including my cell phone and clothing. With the same energy that I once dedicated to my adult film career, I was now focused wholly on getting clean and sober and healthy for my baby.

Craig didn't take the news well, as I knew he wouldn't. I'd met him through my makeup artist and close friend Steve. Steve met Craig, a male model and actor, at a video shoot at this beautiful mansion that apparently belonged to Craig's ex-girlfriend. I don't think she even knew about it. She was out of town and he rented her house out. Steve said Craig was the most beautiful man he had ever met and he couldn't stop talking about him.

My transsexual friend Sylvia also had lots of great things to say about Craig. I met Sylvia through Steve, and the two of us used to hang out at her place to watch *Jerry Springer.* She was also friends with Craig, who use to sell weed to her. One day, I dropped an autographed photograph of myself off at her house. Craig saw it on her refrigerator and told her he wanted to meet me.

I was dating someone else at the time, but we got into a fight one night when Sylvia told me about a party where

Craig would be. She planned to stay home but thought I should go meet him.

I did. And all the hype about him was not exaggerated. When he walked in, I literally caught my breath. He was the best-looking man I'd ever seen and I was literally dumbstruck by his beauty. He was tall and an interesting mix of Irish and Spanish. It was not surprising to learn he was a Calvin Klein model and that he starred in a popular soap opera.

Despite his breathtaking beauty, my boyfriend still had my heart.

Not too long after, Craig got my number and called to say he wanted to see me again. By then, my boyfriend and I had finally broken up for good, so I agreed to the date. I lived in Santa Monica at the time, so I told him I'd meet him in LA. We got a hotel room and got drunk. The next day I left wearing his flannel shirt.

When he called me again, I told him that I didn't want to meet for another drunk hookup. If he wanted to see me, he had to come to my place for dinner, sober. I wanted to spend a night getting to know him. He drove over on his motorcycle, but he wasn't sober. Apparently, he had been secretly drinking the whole time, and when he finally passed out, a whole bottle of vodka slipped out of his pants. We didn't have sex that night, but in the morning, he grabbed me and we were intimate. Two times was all it took. Flash forward: now I'm pregnant and in rehab.

I had bigger issues on my mind than worrying about how Craig would take this. First off, I had to learn to once again live sober. The first thing they taught us in rehab was to establish a routine. This meant getting up in the morning at 6 a.m., making our bed, having breakfast, and going through a series of therapies and group sessions. If you missed breakfast, you were out of luck. Same for lunch and dinner. Then we had a snack and were locked in at 10 p.m. until the next morning. The idea was to help us re-establish our circadian rhythms that had been wiped out by drug and alcohol binges.

Getting sober was a full-time job and very humbling. I found it oddly peaceful to be able to shut out the world and let go of everyday stressors. It was heaven, not being tethered to my cell phone or worrying about my career or where I'd get my next drugs from.

I was under no illusion that I wanted to be with Craig or that the three of us would make a family. I knew him for what he was: a drunk and a womanizer. But I felt so blessed to have this child growing in my belly. I was completely alone in LA, with my family far away, and I felt like God had given me this little angel to help guide me through this crazy world.

After my third month in the facility, I was moved into a group home in Orange County with six other women. I had my own bedroom and was expected to find a job. Obviously, my former career was no longer an option. I'd never had a real job before, apart from working at Burger King and a couple of clothing stores.

One of my AA sponsors worked for a mortgage company and recommended me for a telemarketing job at the firm. Some people hated cold calling, but I loved it and was good at it. After my first week, I was getting up to 10 to 20 leads a day for the mortgage broker, where others weren't getting any. I was able to effortlessly get a social security number from a potential customer, which impressed my boss enough that he made me team leader. I had always done well in clothing sales because I was a closer, always working hard for a better life.

I advanced from team lead to running the office. When someone got stuck on a script, I'd step in to help them close their call. This earned me a bit of a commission from the loan officer. Soon though, I got tired of seeing them make all the money and decided to take some courses to become a mortgage broker.

Meanwhile, I lived in a sober living house and continued working on staying sober and healthy. Over the past months, I had called Craig to tell him about the baby, but he wouldn't acknowledge it was his. Finally, in my eighth month, he came to visit me at rehab, but he still wasn't very receptive. He also didn't recognize me. When I went into rehab, I must have weighed about 110 pounds. Now, thanks to a healthy diet – and a new addiction for double cheeseburgers – my weight skyrocketed up to 190 pounds.

I was healthy and eating well. I really enjoyed living in the house among the other women, all of whom were working hard to turn our lives around. Sobriety is a precarious thing, as I learned the hard way. Addiction is always there, lurking just around the corner and waiting for you to slip.

All of our worlds were rocked one day when one of our counselors overdosed in the bathroom. I was the one who found her, and I was shocked. This woman had been clean for 27 years; she had toured the world leading seminars about her sobriety, and just like that, all that hard work – and her life – was gone. This happened the night before I was due to go into labor and it really hit me hard. I looked back on my own life and saw how depressing and dark that lifestyle actually was. I wanted to do better. I felt that God had given me this second chance, and I wasn't about to blow it.

My oldest son was born on October 15th, 1998. Because I gained so much weight, the doctor brought me in a day early. After being induced and having a painful labor, I gave birth. My son was the most beautiful baby I'd ever seen, and he shocked me with his full head of dark, straight hair. He was also very white, prompting the nurses to keep checking my toe tag every time they brought him to me for nursing, to the point where it really got annoying and I told them to just give me my baby.

He was absolutely perfect, and I don't believe I've ever felt as happy as I did the day he was born. I would hold him for hours and just stare at him and take in his lilac smell. It was everything I dreamed about since I was a little girl playing with dolls, imagining my future family.

My old boyfriend, Danny, was the first to visit me and meet my son. He had come back into my life, and two weeks before I delivered, he put me up in a room at a hotel in Santa Monica. I think he hoped he was the father and wanted us to be a family.

I never felt as if I would've met Craig if it wasn't for my relationship with Danny. Everything about him really amazed me, but I entered his life during a time when he was lonely and as shut down as I was at the time.

He hid behind his music. It didn't help that he had a co-writer who despised me and saw me as a distraction. Danny would tuck me away in his bedroom while he was recording downstairs, then sneak up to eat dinner or lunch with me. Sometimes I would only see him for an hour a day. When I got bored, I wanted to escape into my old world where I always found trouble.

This is what Danny feared the most about me. He wanted to protect me. One of the ways he'd look out for me was by sending his friend David Paul to look out for me. David had a brother named Peter Paul. They were both bodybuilders and famous actors who did a slew of films in the '80s called *Barbarians*.

David would come and get me and take me to a Gold's Gym in Venice. Once, I remember Kobe Bryant pulling into the gym parking lot in his pickup with music banging.

Everyone in the gym would crowd around David like he was a god. He could never even get his workout in with all the people swarming him. David would entertain me while Danny worked.

Even though we were broken up at the time, Danny really wanted to be there for my son. He was the first person at the hospital. When I got out of the hospital, he bought me a new car and remained a steadfast presence in my life until he died of an accidental drowning in 2015.

Craig, however, was not ready for the baby to arrive. When I went into labor, I called him from the hospital. Later, I learned that it freaked him out so much that he had drunk a bottle of Jack Daniels and passed out. The next day, he showed up with a girl who questioned his paternity and said that all biracial babies look like everyone.

Regardless, Craig was the first person to be photographed with our son and seemed to warm to the idea of being a father. When I got out of the hospital, I returned to the sober living house to finish out the remainder of my treatment, and Craig invited me and my son to move in with him while I found my own place.

I knew this was a bad idea for a variety of reasons. For starters, the two of us didn't even know one another well. On top of this was Craig's drinking and womanizing. He wasn't ready for a kid, but at the same time, he said he wanted to try to be a good father. Right away, it was clear it wasn't going to work. Newly sober, I didn't want to be around people who still drank and did drugs, and Craig was showing no signs of stopping. I had never met a hardcore alcoholic before, and it was troubling to be around. One of his friends even questioned why I would let Craig drive around with the baby in his car, because he was always drunk.

I ended up renting the house next door to Craig's and moving out after a couple of days.

Meanwhile, Craig continued his drinking and womanizing. I didn't realize the extent of the latter until I got a visit from one of my close friends, fellow adult film star Alicia Rio. The baby was two weeks old when she came over with Ray, the guy she was dating.

I knew that Craig was a big fan of hers. She was Latina and Craig was fluent in Spanish, so the two of them engaged in their own private conversation while Ray and I watched in silence. They continued to flirt throughout the visit, and then finally, the couple left, with Alicia leaving me one of her business cards with her phone number so I could call her.

The next day, I took our son out for a walk in the stroller. When I got home, I realized Alicia's card was not where she left it on the table. I went over to Craig's to talk to him about it and heat up a bottle for the baby. He wasn't home, and immediately, I knew he had to be with her. Sure enough, when I hit redial on his phone, it went straight to Alicia. The two of them were together. My friend of over a decade and the father of my child had betrayed me.

I felt sick, hurt, and just broken. When Craig stopped by my house later, he'd been drinking heavily. He asked to see our son, but I wouldn't let him in the house because he was drunk. He was irrational and denied being with Alicia, which led to a huge fight. He ended up calling the cops. He told them I wouldn't let him in to see his son and he was afraid of my harming him.

The police showed up, banging at my door. I thought it was Craig at first, so I didn't answer. When I finally let them in, one of the cops threw me down on the floor and busted my head before snatching the baby out of my arms. Craig told them all about my former profession, and between that and being a Black woman, I felt the full extent of the police's discrimination.

They ended up arresting me for an unpaid jaywalking ticket from two years earlier that I didn't even remember I had. They carted me off to jail while Craig was sent home. Because he was so drunk, the police called protective services to take the baby.

Just like that. At two weeks old, my son entered the system, one that I would continue to fight. He'd been ripped out of my arms and my heart was broken.

I sat in jail for several days with nobody local to call and no idea where my son had been taken. Finally, I called my mother in West Virginia to fly out to LA to help me. Once out of jail, I found out where my son had been placed and went to visit him. It nearly broke my soul. I felt a pain I'd never felt before and didn't even know existed. It crushed my heart and spirit, like someone had just reached into my body and snatched my soul.

If jail was bad, it was nothing compared to going to court before Superior Court Commissioner Scott Gordon. This was the same judge who placed Britney Spears under an involuntary conservatorship at the request of her father in 2008; the conservatorship lasted until 2021.

As I did all those years earlier when I appeared on the *People's Court,* I felt like my profession was on trial. The legal system does not smile down on women in the adult film industry. I tried to explain my side of the story: how Craig had been drunk and I didn't want him near my son in that inebriated condition. It had been a verbal altercation, I said, and I was there for a jaywalking ticket, not anything I'd done that night.

I could see it plainly in the judge's eyes: judgment for and condemnation of what I did for a living. I was a porn star. When he looked at me, he saw all the stereotypes and preconceptions of girls in this business.

In the world's eyes, we're damaged, fucked up people with issues and baggage that led us there. People don't see the girls who are working themselves through college because they come from nothing, or the women who are just trying to support themselves, or the girls like me who came from loving homes but got into the industry because they were about to lose their homes.

We're not bad people. We're not monsters. But try standing in front of a judge and speaking up for yourself. It's a downhill battle that I sorely lost and continue to fight to this day.

After several weeks, I was finally granted a visit with my son in foster care. The look of confusion on his face was horrendous. Even today, I can't stop crying thinking about it, because I felt like I hadn't even been given the chance to grieve his absence. I knew I had to take immediate action and toughen up so that I could get my son back home.

He remained in foster care for six months. Meanwhile, they threw everything at me, from drug therapy and counseling to parenting and conflict classes to more counseling and more parenting classes. I did it all, whatever they asked. All the while, the social worker seemed to stack up more and more things against me from my past as an excuse not to give my son back. Finally, I met all their criteria and they had no choice except to return my son home.

He was 10 months old at that point and had spent more time away from me than with me. He had already started to walk. I missed all of the milestones that a first-time mother should experience at home.

I was determined never to let that happen again. The two of us became inseparable, and he was such a good little boy. If he woke up before I did in the morning, he would put his *Blues Clues* video in the VCR and watch until my eyes opened.

In the meantime, Craig and Alicia announced they were getting married and wanted full custody of our son. I didn't think I could hurt anymore but they proved me wrong. Not only did my close friend sleep with my boyfriend and betray me, but now she consciously made the decision to fight me for custody of my son.

Craig got into a fight with Alicia while intoxicated and ended up going to jail. He was looking at a fairly lengthy jail sentence and reached out to me for help. He asked if I would hire an attorney to help him fight the sentence.

I thought helping him would mean a better life for my son; I didn't want him to grow up without knowing his father. It was clear that Craig and I would never be together as a couple, but he was still the father of my son, and I thought it would be better if Craig and I were both present in his life.

I helped him and hired an attorney. It was the beginning of a bitter relationship that never worked. He'd spend the next decade getting drunk and calling DCFS to try to get my son taken out of the house.

Craig and Alicia broke up, but it would be decades before I spoke to her again. She died in January 2022 from COVID-related complications at age 55. We'd just begun talking, and she had apologized for her role in the custody fight and for sleeping with Craig. She'd been in a really self-centered time of her life, she said, and had only been thinking about herself and regretted it deeply. I forgave her. We were at different places in our lives and we were young. I had to realize that neither of us was the people we were all those years ago. I'm sure she had no idea the chain reaction that sleeping with Craig would entail.

Over the next several years, police officers and social workers would turn up at my house to drug test me because Craig would report my having parties and fellow porn stars at the house. Long after I left the industry, the harassment would continue. DCFS always answered Craig's calls and seemed determined to take my children away.

I once asked a case worker if the same scrutiny would be placed on me if I were a white woman working an office job. No, she said. My lifestyle and profession definitely put a target on my back. After she retired, she told me that she'd never seen anyone so harassed.

The whole situation drove me to move to San Francisco to start a new career and life with my son. I sent him to live with my mom so I could get my shit together.

It turned out to be one crazy summer.

Once in San Francisco, I was at a party with a friend. I met a guy that I thought was very sexy. He presented himself like a boss man and showered me with expensive gifts. We went on a lot of elaborate shopping sprees together. Little did I know he was not the man I thought he was, and boy, did I find that out the hard way.

The day started out like many others. It was sunny and we were in downtown San Francisco shopping. We'd been out all day and it was starting to get dark. As we were driving home, I saw his eyes starting to dart around like he was paranoid. Then he suddenly parked the curb on a residential street and jumped out, saying he had to stop to talk to his brother.

All of the sudden, out of nowhere, I looked up through the window and saw police helicopters shining their lights down on the car. Before I could process what was happening, I heard someone screaming at me to freeze and put my hands up in the air where they could see them.

At least 10 federal undercover agents stormed the car, screaming at me to get out of the vehicle as I yelled, "Don't shoot!" My legs were shaking as I slid out of the passenger seat. The agents quickly grabbed me and hurled me down on the ground on my stomach.

They seemed unconcerned that I was wearing a midriff Playboy Bunny shirt and that my bare skin was scraping the pavement. Then they helped me to my feet and escorted me to the back of the police car as they raided the guy's trunk, pulling out kilos of cocaine.

I tried to ask what was going on but was instructed to shut up. They then took me to the station and threw me into a cell where I could see a group of officers huddled over a computer screen, talking in soft voices.

After a few minutes, I was led into an interrogation room as if I was wanted for murder. The agent in charge explained that they'd been trailing this guy for several weeks and that he was a major drug lord. They wanted to know how long

I'd known him and where we met. I explained I hadn't been dating him long and that I met him at a party.

I told them I had no idea that this guy was a drug dealer and that I was an unwitting, innocent bystander. After I said my peace, I started to get pissed. Why was I the one being interrogated when they'd been looking for him?

"Why didn't you fuckers get him when he got out of the car?" I wanted to know.

They said they were trying to build a case against him, but in the meantime, I was the one being taken down. They questioned me for hours before explaining I was being held for felony drug possession. I'd done nothing.

When they found out what I did for a living, one of the detectives asked me what it was like to be a famous porn star. It was crazy.

I was held on a million-dollar bail until my court date, when it was reduced and a friend was able to bail me out.

All I kept thinking was how glad I was that my son was with my mother in West Virginia. I thanked the holy stars that he was not here to witness this.

I showed up for court wearing a tailored two-piece designer suit. I was sitting in the front row of the courtroom when a guy leaned over the wooden railing separating the galley from the courtroom area. He looked a lot like Johnny Depp in *21 Jump Street*; I thought he was hot. He asked me whom I was there to defend, obviously mistaking me for a lawyer.

I explained I was actually a plaintiff and there to defend myself. Without hesitating, he jumped over the railing and sat down next to me.

I asked him if he was a cop. Yes, he said. Not just a cop but an undercover agent. I was shocked to learn he was actually there to testify in my case. I was completely shocked.

He went up to the judge's bench and grabbed my case, quickly scanning the notes. He returned to say that they weren't planning to charge me for the felony because they realized I was innocent.

He had a very charming demeanor that I found sexy. I gave him my number and we started dating. I really enjoyed his company and was amazed by his work. Some nights, he would come over to my house after working a sting. He often dressed up like a homeless guy and panhandled in shitty areas of town. They'd situate him outside a drug-infested building in the Tenderloin district where he shook a can for money. He was wired most of the time, and he was amazed at what people would say when they were going in and out of drug houses.

I was very intrigued by his doing that kind of work. The job required him to be a sort of actor, and he was good at it. He'd even wear makeup with a fake beard and dirty clothes to look the part.

The summer was nearing an end and my oldest son was due to be back home with me. I was excited about where this relationship was going and told him so one night before he went out to do a job. I never saw him again. He was shot while doing a raid.

I was absolutely freaked out and took it as a sign that I needed to get the hell out of San Francisco.

My mother flew Dylan out to me as I packed up my apartment and prepared to move back to LA. My son was almost three. I was eager to find my footing and was in the process of staging a comeback into adult films when tragedy shook my world yet again.

I heard about the plane crash on the news. The charter flight out of the Bahamas had been carrying 22-year-old singer Aaliyah and her entourage when it went down one minute after takeoff in August 2001. All nine passengers – including the pilot – died.

I knew that my hairdresser and best friend Anthony Dodd's friend Eric Foreman had been on the flight and immediately called Anthony to console him. He didn't answer. My heart sank. He was on that plane, too. Worse yet, he somehow survived the crash but died on the way to the hospital.

I was devastated. I had just spoken to Anthony about changing my image. We were in the process of helping me make a comeback in the acting world and doing more music videos. I'd even given him a car because he was always late to our early morning hair appointments.

My son and I attended Anthony's funeral. So many celebrities were there, with Deborah Coxx singing at the

Ebenezer Baptist Church, the same church my vocal coach, Seth Riggs, sent me to hear the choir years earlier. I got up and spoke at the funeral with my son by my side. I told funny stories about Anthony and how he would always tell me, "BIYATCH, I have put the longest weaves in your head, and you are the only bitch wearing hair that long – you and Cher."

Despite the levity of my stories, I was barely able to stand. My tears just would not stop. Death hit me hard. At this point, I had lost my grandmother and uncle and it nearly broke me. I never imagined I would lose Anthony, too. My son did not understand why his mother was in such pain.

My life changed after Anthony's death. We moved to a condo in Beverly Hills where my son began acting oddly. He told me that he was seeing things in the home that were scaring him. One night, he woke up and swore that someone was in his room. I didn't see anything. At first, I thought he was just acting out because he missed his father, but he would point and move his finger as if following someone or something through the room. I asked him to draw me a picture of what he was seeing but he never did.

I was in a dark place following the loss of my friend and because of the void in my career. I knew I needed help, so I asked my aunt to come and get Dylan, because I worried he was going through a hard time. I thought he needed to be in a family environment while I got my life back on track. She flew out to LA and the two of them headed back to Atlanta on September 10th, 2001.

Watching him get on that plane was one of the harder things I'd ever done, but I knew I needed to get my life together so I could be strong for him. I knew it was the best decision at the time, and after I dropped them at the airport, I went home and slept the rest of the day.

I woke early the next day to the sound of my phone ringing off the hook. It was my mother. Had I heard the news? Did I see the Twin Towers? I was still groggy, and her words weren't making any sense. I asked her what she was talking about to which she replied, "Have you been on fucking Mars?"

I turned on the news, saw the crumbling towers, and learned about the terrorists and the planes. I immediately called my aunt to check on my son. They'd made it home safely, but our lives would never be the same.

13

CANDY STRIPING

Once you've been in the adult film and sex industries, it's hard to transition over to a normal life. That's just the way it is. Like it or not, the stigma of the sex industry embeds itself on you like a tattoo. Even when you try to leave, you never entirely get away.

I saw this with some of my friends, though it certainly isn't impossible to leave the industry. One adult film star I knew became an attorney. Another friend and former porn star, Mimi Miyagi, even ran for mayor of Las Vegas. But even when you transition into a different career, the label follows you into that life. I get it; it's a dark business and a lot of people see us as either novelties or less than human.

Doing adult films and escorting was something I told myself I had been doing to survive as a single mom to support my family. At the same time, I was paying a cost for that lifestyle, and I knew I needed a change and wanted to do something better for my children. I also wanted to have the type of "normal" family I'd dreamed of having for my entire life.

I thought back to myself as that little girl playing with her dolls, being by a strict grandmother who really loved her. I missed that unconditional love. Like my grandmother and my mother before me, I was raising three kids on my own as a single mother. I'd spent all those years trying to build the family I wanted. My problem was that I'd always chosen the wrong men. Men with mommy issues. Narcissists. Guys that liked to throw my past in my face even though they'd just met me. I'd spent years trying to break out of the industry and just wanted to be a part of normal society. A good person. A good mom. Someone who cares about her family and just wants to be able to support them.

But once you're in the business, you'll always be a porn star. Your films and magazine centerfolds are out there for anyone to see. This does not disappear, which is something that younger women entering the industry need to understand. It's nearly impossible to swab your Internet presence. One of my friends was able to pull all of her stuff off the Internet, but at an incredible cost, and she hadn't done nearly as many films as I had, nor had she been inducted into the Porn Star Hall of Fame.

I knew my past would always be there but was prepared to transition into a new line of work. I knew the money wouldn't be the same, but given the trade-offs, it just meant downsizing my spending habits.

During my first pregnancy, I worked as a mortgage broker. I had liked the work, so I decided to take a position selling insurance policies to elderly people. The job was arduous yet fulfilling. Part of the job meant working with elderly people to help manage their insurance plans. As I worked with them one-on-one, it became clear that there were large holes in communication and their understandings of their health ailments and medications. Many simply couldn't afford the pills they were being prescribed. Others were struggling to even understand basic health concepts surrounding their diagnoses.

It became clear there was an enormous disconnect between the healthcare providers and elderly patients when it came to understanding what medications were being prescribed for their various ailments or why. Many who couldn't afford their prescriptions told me they were cutting their pills in half. At that point, my understanding of healthcare was also limited, so I really couldn't help them manage outside of explaining how a particular policy might help. It broke my heart to see all of these vulnerable people with no one to look after them.

I began to feel my humanity come back. Working in the sex industry hardened something inside of me as I tamped down emotions in favor of dollar signs. I had become a hard-nosed businesswoman intent on making money and disconnecting from other humans in a way that viewed them as transactional. I hadn't realized my heart was so scabbed over until my elderly clients reminded me of what's important in life: love, humanity, and using one's skills to help others. It was life-changing, really, and I felt grateful for this insight that would ultimately change the course of my career and bring me closer to my true self.

I quit the job and signed up for nursing school. I thought I had the right mixture of compassion and cool-headed temperament for nursing and I really wanted to do something to help these elderly people navigate their health concerns. Nursing would also provide a stable life and respectable career. In 2011, I enrolled at Casa Loma College. I was in my 40s, decades older than most of the students, and I felt so out of place among the young kids fresh out of high school.

These feelings of intimidation continued when, on the first day of school, one of our professors directed us to read the first six chapters in the book, explaining we would be tested the following day. I began to panic, and my first question to the teacher was, "Which paragraphs and particular subjects we were going to be tested on?" The answer was not forthcoming, and I realized I had a real challenge ahead. It had been years since I'd been in school, and my past drug use had no doubt killed off more than a few brain cells.

It was a huge learning curve to get myself back in the groove. My last two years of high school in West Virginia had been a wash at best. After I was emancipated and got my own apartment, I was more concerned with my part-time jobs and being able to pay my own bills. This left little time for school, so I'd basically get up a couple of hours before my last class and cram in as much studying as I could. Back then, I was so tired from work that I barely squeaked through. Now, I had to teach myself to study again and focus on the task at hand.

Harder yet was the fact that my entire schedule had been turned upside down. I was going to school five days a week while raising three children. This required enormous organizational skills and led to a deficit of sleep. The hardest part was finding time to study. I would cook dinner, put the kids to bed around 8:30 p.m., then start cramming. I would then sleep for a couple of hours before getting the kids up and ready for school. It was the same fatigue I felt as a girl cramming before class, but the difference now was that I had three children to support.

This went on for four semesters, followed by clinicals in hospitals throughout LA. Despite the grueling schedule and lack of sleep, I found my new life incredibly rewarding and was doing really well in school. I ended up graduating at the top of my class, but not without my past creeping up to haunt me.

This happened in a couple of ways. Once, during a clinical, my fellow students and I had to give a man a bath. The patient ended up getting an erection, and I couldn't even look at him because I was so embarrassed. I felt like everyone was staring at me, as irrational as it may sound. I'm sure it was a reflex, but it was as if my worlds started to collide. I was sensitive to my past and wondered how many people recognized me as Domonique Simone.

That question was answered soon enough.

At the time, I wasn't a big fan of social media, but I did have a Facebook page, primarily to keep in contact with family members and childhood friends back in West Virginia and Georgia. Every once in a while, however, someone from the industry would sneak in between the cracks. After a point, I realized that several of my former adult film stars were now on my page. I didn't have a problem with that; they were my friends. Over time, my page started to become more centered around those friends from the entertainment industry. It didn't matter; I knew it was only a matter of time before my classmates discovered I used to be an adult film star.

A guy named Juanito figured it out first. Apparently, he was a huge porn fan and recognized me from one of my films. At the time, we were doing a clinical in the paraplegic department. The patients in that wing used the most amazing technology to blow into a wand that would manipulate their computers to perform a variety of functions. Suddenly, all of the clients were asking me to grab things from their shelves.

It turned out that Juanito and some of the other male students had told the patients all about my former career as a porn star and they'd uploaded several of my movies onto their computers. Let's just say there was a lot of blowing going on in that place.

One of the patients finally said something to me about it. That transgression was a big deal to me, and I got called into the board of the nursing department's office. The head of the department's name was Miss B. Bridges, whom I learned was related to the actor Todd Bridges by marriage. Barbara was outraged by Juanito's behavior and the fact that he'd necessarily revealed my past to the patients for his own entertainment.

I later found out the cat had been out of the bag for some time, though nobody had the decency or guts to tell me. I felt so ashamed, and I often thought that the students were secretly making fun of me.

I felt violated, but then again, that's the price you pay. You can never undo your past once it's out there. It was really discouraging, though, to think that Juanito had gone to the trouble just to try to embarrass me in front of my fellow students and patients.

Juanito got kicked out of the program, but this didn't make me feel any better. In fact, I had a lot of guilt about it. Juanito was one semester away from graduating and might have made a great nurse. In the end, however, it wasn't my decision.

After I graduated, I went to work as a nurse. It was exhausting and emotional work. It was so sad seeing people who had been abandoned by their kids left to die in a hospital. I constantly thought of my grandmother. On one hand, I was happy to be helping others, but on the other, it was draining to deal with death at work and then go home to a whole slew of other problems.

No matter what I did, despite the fact that I'd changed professions, the stigma of my earlier life never wore off. Even now, after retiring from the adult business and trying to lead a normal life, I still feel as if I am being judged.

A couple of incidents stick out. One day, I took my daughter to her daycare while I attended nursing classes. When I picked her back up, the supervisor called me into the office and told me that someone had emailed explicit pictures of me to her. I broke down crying because I always felt like the other parents were judging me. Even though I was dressed in scrubs, it was upsetting that everyone at the school knew that I used to do adult films.

The same thing happened at my son's school. At the time, he was 13 years old, and I went to pick him up after school. The principal stopped me to say that someone had walked into his office to drop off a packet with several explicit photos of me. The principal, however, called that person out on why they were trying to embarrass me and what that said about their motivations. "No matter what you did in your past," the principal said, "that's not the person I see when you come to pick up your son.

Even worse were the years of being harassed by the

Department of Children and Family Services (DCFS), whom we called "Black CPS."

There was a hotline that anyone could call to report an incident, whether it was true or not. I didn't have great relationships with the fathers of my children and also had a few people in my life who wanted nothing more than to do me harm and harass me. If DCFS received a complaint, they would sometimes show up at my house in the middle of the night when I was sleeping. Once, they and the police turned up on my doorstep at 3 a.m. DCFS agents used to come to my home, jump on my balcony, and peek through my blinds to see if I was home; they accused me of dodging them and not opening my door when I simply was not at home.

When you are on their radar, it's hard to get off. Once, I got called into the office to be shown pictures of myself in various sex acts laid out all over the desk. The DCFS worker asked me what these were, and I said, "Well, they appear to be pictures of myself. You guys knew that I was in the adult film business, so if you can't tell what it is, then I think that something is truly wrong."

She then told me that the photos didn't appear to be from a photoshoot, but they looked like they had been shot in someone's private home. I stared at her dumbfounded. How do you defend yourself?

"Do you see me dressed like that right now?" I asked. "I'm standing in front of you with my nursing scrubs on, so what is your problem?"

She accused me of making porn films in front of my children, as the complaint had alleged. This led to workers interviewing my children, asking sexually explicit questions about whether they'd ever seen me naked or performing sex acts. By the time my children were in grade school, they were to people coming over to talk to them about my personal life.

It was unrelenting. I told the DCFS worker that I was tired of being judged by their department. They had already put me through so much and dragged me through the dirt.

The icing on the cake was the time I was accused of giving a blow job to a male DCFS agent in exchange for a favorable report. Apparently, the man accepted sexual favors from another African American woman in my neighborhood who tested positive for drugs and begged him not to report it.

Because I lived within his jurisdiction – despite never having met him – the department assumed that I was the client in question. The client's name was eventually released in the media, but the damage had already been done. They never apologized, but they did send my file to a secure server assigned for celebrity cases in order to avoid workers having easy access to the system. They did this to prevent leaks in the media and the press from getting ahold of personal data.

It was completely unfair; the cards were stacked against me.

Mind you, I was not the only adult performer to be harassed by this system whose purpose is supposedly to protect children. It is a system that vows to keep families together, but it actually tears them apart. It's a system that has failed so many children and has been sued by several families for negligence and wrongdoing. Some children have been sexually assaulted in foster homes or left to die from uninvestigated claims. Still, DCFS would come to my home every other day about my alleged drug use, which led to me being subjected to two to three drug screenings a week.

Another problem I had as a former adult film star was people recognizing me out in public. As I mentioned, I'm a very shy person, and I would sometimes go to Hollywood to see my close friend and hair and makeup artist, Steve. I would get recognized all the time, possibly because of my signatory hairstyle: straight bangs and long black hair. The worst part was having creepy men come up to say they recognized me and ask if they knew me from somewhere. It happened a few times when I was out with my family. It was such an invasion of privacy.

Fans don't respect boundaries and would frequently come up to me to say hi or ask for my autograph, even when I was out having dinner with my kids or running errands. Some of the guys would get really aggressive, too, if I ignored them. They would act like they knew me and were entitled to my time. This is why celebrities hide. It's an invasion of privacy. Fans don't get that we're human; we just want to do what we want to do without being noticed.

If I were a pop or R&B musician and someone wanted to take a picture with me, I would do so without making a big deal. But that's not what these guys wanted. They wanted to talk about the ladies I'd been filmed with in various adult films and tell me which sex scenes they liked to see me in. It was an inappropriate conversation and completely embarrassing in front of my kids.

Even worse was when my teenage son's friends recognized me from my films. My son found out about my adult video history when he was about 10. His father told him, which made me very upset. I wanted to wait until my children were mature enough to understand. That didn't happen, and it caused a lot of grief between me and my son when he was in high school.

I didn't realize how prevalent porn is among high school boys and how easily it is accessed over the Internet. It was way different during my time, when the Internet was still in its infancy and adult films were purchased or rented from video stores with discretion. That wasn't the case during my son's teen years. Little did I know that his friends were watching my films and calling me the "hot mom."

My son was popular in high school; he was an athlete and active on the football and track teams. I let him drive my Lamborghini to school; he had a good life, except where I was concerned. He wasn't ashamed of my past as an adult film star, but he really resented that his friends would ogle me. A few of them even went so far as to hit on me. It was embarrassing for both of us, but he took it to heart.

Once, when I took him out to an In-N-Out Burger after a football game, his phone blew up with messages from his friends wanting to know the name of the "hot girl" he was sitting with. He was horrified and pissed. Quite frankly, I was, too.

When I entered the business, the consequences of my choices on my future life didn't even dawn on me, let alone the fact that I would one day have children who would also have to bear this responsibility. I was young and naively didn't take into account the impact my adult film career would have on my life.

It wore thin on all of us, but particularly my oldest son, who hated that part of me and my past.

He railed on me, demanding to know why I had children in the first place, since my past would only ruin their lives. I understood this to a point, but at the same time, his accusations infuriated me. I told him that when I was making films, I wasn't thinking about him being in high school; I did what I did because I had to take care of him, his brother, and his sister. I reminded him that his life wasn't bad. He didn't want for anything, and most of all, he had my unconditional love.

I think all teenagers are embarrassed by their parents in one way or another, but even more so for a kid whose mom used to be a porn star. I get that, but even mothers are entitled to their pasts, and it was never going to be easy for either of us to make peace with my past. All we could do was move forward.

Graduation Pic Nursing School

14

THE COST OF BEAUTY

I slapped the nurse's hands as she struggled to clamp the oxygen mask over my mouth. I could feel the vomit rising in my throat and tried to push her hands away. It wasn't her fault. She had no idea I was aspirating and was just trying to do her job. My lungs were in the middle of collapsing and I felt like I was drowning. I fought back like a wild demon. My last thought as I drifted off was that I'd forgotten to tell anyone where I was.

It was supposed to be a straightforward, relatively simple cosmetic procedure. That morning, I went into a plastic surgeon's office to have a tummy tuck and liposuction. It was March 2017, and I was 45 years old. After a lifetime of obsessing over my body, I was having trouble shedding the weight after the birth of my third child. A little plastic surgery would do the trick, I reasoned, as it always had in the past.

After I woke up from the anesthesia, however, my blood saturation levels were not going up. They prefer a range somewhere in the 90s, but mine hovered near 80. The nurse was hesitant to let me go home, so they checked me into a local hospital. Already, I was having a hard time breathing. The tummy tuck had bunched all my organs together, and it hurt to breathe. Then they gave me Demerol and I had an allergic reaction, making me throw up. By the time I rang for the nurse, my lungs gave in and I slipped into an induced coma.

I only told a couple of people in my life that I was having surgery: a friend who was watching my place, and, oddly, the man who'd broken my heart 20 years ago, Ryan. Out of the blue, I found him on Facebook and called him. It was really late, but to my surprise, he answered, and we made plans to talk when I got home. I was so relieved to find him that I got down on my knees and prayed, thanking God for helping me find the love of my life. It would be a week until I talked to him, and he would have no idea what had happened to me.

Likewise, my three children didn't know. They were with their fathers, and I didn't feel the need to worry them about the surgical procedure. My daughter's birthday gifts were sitting at my house waiting to be delivered. I had no idea what day it was or how long I'd been asleep.

It was the strangest feeling, being in an unconscious state. I was dreaming about everyday life, doing errands. I would get in my car and drive to the bank and try to deposit a check in the drive-through, but I was the only person there.

The lights were on, but no employees were working. The streets were unnervingly quiet; no joggers or pedestrians waiting at bus stops, no other cars on the road. It was just me in this gauzy, half-awake world.

In my coma state, I dreamt I was trying to get to my kids. I was desperate to find them but crippled by fear. Outside, everything was pitch dark and I was afraid of falling into the water because I didn't know how to swim. Instead, I dropped bags of groceries down the stairs of a house I didn't recognize (oddly, I would later end up buying a house just like it).

I remember seeing a white light, almost like sunlight in the clouds, and being drawn to it. I have no idea what happens when we die, but I knew I was in trouble. I felt like I had transitioned to the other side as I was increasingly drawn to that light. Along with the brightness, I also had visions of complete darkness. It was the type of dark that felt like being in a cave; I couldn't even see my hand in front of me.

I woke to a nurse uncoiling a tube out of my mouth. A young respiratory therapist started crying when he saw me open my eyes. He told me it was just like being in an episode of *ER*. As he cried, I realized how close I'd come to dying. Apparently, I coded a few times and they were close to writing me off.

I'd been in a coma for almost nine days, the doctor explained. I touched my short hair and asked what happened to my wig.

"You threw up on it," he said, "so we took it away."

I started laughing in relief. It felt like a fitting metaphor for inane vanity. I couldn't believe how grateful I felt to still be here. I'd made it back from the other side. It was a life-changing moment for me and I knew I needed to get my shit together. It would take another month of in-house physical therapy to relearn basic functions like breathing and walking again. I had to ask a friend to deliver my daughter's birthday gifts.

God had given me a second chance, and I wasn't about to throw it away. I needed to clean up my act and stop letting vanity put my life in jeopardy. I needed to get my life together, stop undergoing all these procedures, and be there for my children.

That's the thing about being in the sex industry: your body is everything. It's hard to give that up when you're used to making money off your image.

The plastic surgeon who enlarged my breasts and redid my nose, Dr. Wesley G. Harline, later had a slew of malpractice lawsuits against him, stemming from the early 1990s, when I had my work done. Two of the lawsuits were for allegedly using silicone in breast implants after the moratorium on silicone by the FDA in 1992. Other women sued him for reportedly enlarging their breasts too much while others alleged the doctor punctured lungs during procedures, according to a 1996 article in the *Deseret News*.

That same article said the state had been investigating

Harline on and off for the past two decades and filed a petition alleging he had used inadequate amounts of anesthesia in at least two surgeries, causing patients to wake up during surgery; he even injected silicone into people's faces, among other charges.

None of this was surprising to me, as my own experiences with him had been questionable, but it just speaks to the risks that people in the industry are willing to undergo to further their careers when they don't have the money for reputable doctors in LA.

I had lots of procedures over the years. It was just what people in the industry did.

Sometimes we were downright stupid, like the time Steve convinced me to get discount lip injections. He told me about a plastic surgeon from Mexico who was in town and who did procedures right in a person's home. The doctor was coming over to his place later that day and he asked if I wanted to partake in two-for-one collagen lip treatments for $200.

Steve was always telling me that I had thin, villainous lips, so I got regular injections from my plastic surgeon for $1,000 a treatment. I knew better than to trust a roving witch doctor from Mexico, but Steve wore me down.

Sure enough, this guy even looked like a witch doctor with his big black bag like the priest from the movie *The Exorcist*. He was accompanied by two stern-faced older female assistants who were dressed head-to-toe in shapeless black shifts like stone-face assassins. The trio specialized in drive-by sex change operations that they performed in hotel rooms at a fraction of the cost of those performed by American physicians. I heard of at least one patient dying on their couch.

Steve went first, after which his lips resembled hotdog buns.

"I think his lips are too big," I told the doctor, who assured me it was just the swelling. "He needs to drink arnica tea," he said in a heavy Spanish accent.

Steve's lips were approximately five times the size they were supposed to be. He looked like something out of a cartoon. Somehow, I trusted the doctor when he said that this was normal. Sure enough, when he was done, I could almost feel my upper lip touching the bottom of my nose. When I tried to complain, the doctor once again assured me that the swelling would go down before depositing the used syringes into his bag instead of the trash can.

I was sure we'd both get staph infections. Pissed off, I called my then-husband to come pick me up from Steve's. He started laughing hysterically the second he saw me and I directed him to drive me straight home. I immediately called my plastic surgeon who called in a prescription for Valium. He directed my husband to pick it up and keep me away from the mirror. It was a Thursday; he made me an appointment for Monday. I stayed sedated the entire weekend, worried the witch doctor had injected silicone in my lips, which my doctor explained would be nearly impossible to remove.

I got lucky. It was saline, the cheapest substance the doctor could have used. This was good news, but only slightly. It took a heavy dose of antibiotics and lip radiation to get my lips back to normal.

I immediately went to see Steve, yelling at him about the voodoo motherfucker who had screwed up our lips. Steve was hiding behind a cloth face mask. This was the only time in my life I ever saw him hide any part of his face. We both vowed that was the last time we'd ever get work done by anyone outside of a doctor's office.

It's amazing how many women use doctors like this one to get work done. Many of these doctors fly into LA and set up shop in hotel rooms. I knew a girl who was given hearty doses of painkillers while she got 50 to 100 collagen shots in her ass. Other girls fly to Costa Rica or Mexico to get work done.

Another thing I did was have a doctor sew a mesh patch on my tongue to keep me from eating. The procedure was pretty simple, and it basically forces you onto a liquid diet: if you ate anything, the food would get caught in the mesh and you could possibly pull your tongue off.

After the doctor sewed the mesh on, my tongue was swollen for hours. I remember driving home with Steve afterwards and having a panic attack because it was so swollen and I felt like I couldn't breathe. I rolled down the window and stuck my head out, panting like a dog.

It was a pretty extreme thing to do, but at that point, I had three children and was having a really hard time taking off the weight from my most recent pregnancy. It was also a very difficult time in my life in general because I was in nursing school. Along with the mesh patch, I took Adderall first thing in the morning to do my 12-hour clinicals and drank black coffee all day. I was surviving on a liquid diet of about 200 calories a day.

It worked. I had to limit my calorie intake to 800 calories a day, and it was a pretty hardcore fix for me.

Later, in 2020, I had a butt enhancement by a doctor in Newport Beach, which also didn't go well. I ended up getting an infection and my butt became so inflamed, it started filling up with liquid. This was right around the onset of the pandemic and my doctor was out of the country when I began getting sick. Every time I sat down, I could feel it going "squish, squish squish." It felt like my ass was on fire.

I called a doctor in Santa Monica because I was having a similar problem with one of my breasts. The infection there was spreading through my body. The doctor immediately told me that he had to replace my breast implants because it was so infected, and he needed to look inside to see what was going on.

I went into surgery that day. The streets were almost empty. He was probably one of the only surgeons who was operating at that time because he had his own surgery center. I signed a waiver, and I told him by no means was he to take out the butt implants.

While I was under, he determined they needed to come out.

The doctor spoke to my then-husband and told him it was a life-or-death situation. The implants needed to come out pronto. My husband granted him permission to do what he needed to do. When I woke up after the surgery, I reached behind to grab my butt and it was as flat as a board. I was in shock. When the doctor removed the implant, part of my body tissue came out with it.

He told me that I should undergo these oxygen treatments to help the tissue regenerate, so I went through with them. I had to lay in a hyperbaric machine that reminded me of a six-foot tall, glass coffin. I could watch Netflix or do whatever I wanted to do to remain calm for the hour-long treatment.

Usually I did okay, but one day, my anxiety was triggered. I don't know what set it off, but perhaps it was watching *American Horror Story* on loop. I had been in there for about 30 minutes when I started freaking out and pounding on the glass.

Can you imagine what it feels like to be in a tank and you can't get out? The doctor came over to say he couldn't let me out because if he opened the machine at that moment, my lungs could collapse. It was horrible, just like laying in a closed coffin. I get anxiety just thinking about it now, because it provokes a mortal fear of being stuck in a confined space.

That was one of the most horrifying experiences that I've ever gone through, and I will never forget it for the rest of my life.

The good thing was, one day I woke up, looked in the mirror, and could see that tissue was starting to regenerate in my buttocks. After about two months of treatment, my buttocks were back to normal.

This was all part of the cost of beauty. I learned that you get what you pay for. For my most recent surgery, I went to Dr. Jeffrey Hoefflin, the son of Dr. Steven Hoefflin, who performed some of Michael Jackson's surgeries. Jeffrey cleaned up the shoddy work of past doctors.

After a lifetime of cultivating my image to stay relevant as an adult film actress, I'm trying to learn to grow old gracefully. This means no more plastic surgeries. My most recent surgery was not to augment my breasts but rather to bring them down to a more manageable size. After getting sick with COVID-19 and dealing with complications with my lungs, I wanted to lighten my load by taking 10 pounds off my chest. At one point in my career, I had 2,200 CCs of saline in my breasts, but now I am down to a much more manageable 400 CCs.

It's hard to believe I walked around with that much weight on my chest. Vanity is a strange beast and can lead you in some bad directions, especially when it comes to me.

I'd like to think I was smarter than that at this point in my life, but I'm clearly still learning to stand on my own two feet and trust myself. Still, I'm done making these kinds of reckless mistakes. I can safely say I've closed that chapter of my life and am determined to live more deliberately.

Cost Of Beauty

Cost Of Beauty

15

PHOENIX RISING

My followers on Instagram give me a hard time because I'm obsessed with television from the 1990s. Even today, I watch reruns of shows like *The Fresh Prince of Bel Air* and *The Real World* because it's all new to me. What can I say? The '90s were a blur. I lost a decade and am making up for lost time.

Today, I live in a house in the Hollywood Hills, sheltered from the rest of the world. I have neighbors I've never met and am protected by a security system with multiple cameras that stream on a big wall monitor in my bedroom. Those cameras help me feel safe from the world and my past.

I'm happy to say I'm surrounded by baby books, rattles, and building blocks. In June 2022, I became a mother to my fourth child, Jackson Michael. At 51, I can say that I'm ready to be a mom again. Despite the lack of sleep, I'm so happy to be going through this drama-free. It's a whole different experience without the prying eyes of DCFS harassing me and my children.

After many years of fighting biased judges who held my past against me, I now have custody of all three of my youngest children and am working on rebuilding those relationships.

It's been a while since I have had a small child. When I was pregnant with my first three children, I used to love the smell of Pine Sol and eating ice cream. I laugh with my mother, who is 65 and has a baby girl who is three and another daughter who is 12. She says that when she was pregnant, she liked the smell of gasoline, which probably explains why I'm so crazy.

Today, my relationship with my mother is closer than ever. It's a consolation, and I continue to marvel at how much my life has changed. I've realized that the most important part of my life is staying home and being a mom. I'm happier this way. I have no interest in going out or trying to meet up with men.

Jackson is a good baby, and I enjoy spending my days with him. The connection of his name to his famous counterpart was initially lost on me. I had originally planned on naming him Jax, but my son Jagger suggested Jackson, while my oldest son Dylan requested Michael. I thought the name was absolutely perfect. Jackson just turned eight months old in January and is already getting big.

My life is so different today. Now, I wake up, give Jackson breakfast and turn on *Cocomelon*. I spend the day playing with him and have activities and a schedule.

After losing my other kids to their fathers, we're making amends. My daughter is a dancer and my younger son is studying to be a dentist. My oldest son, Dylan, will soon be working with me in my new company and is an aspiring actor.

This little girl from Georgia has come a long way. Now, I feel my life is coming full circle. Not only do I have a great relationship with my mother, aunt, and younger siblings, but I'm also learning new things about my mom and my biological father and his family. It turns out he comes from a musical family, which helps me understand my own life and passions.

After a career as an adult film actress, escort, mortgage broker, and nurse, I just launched a new career as a music producer this past summer, along with my long-time friend Steve Erhardt. Steve and I have been friends for more than 20 years; he's seen me through some rough times and has always offered me love and support.

In 2022, we put on two concerts with Mary J. Bilge and another featuring El Alfa. Dylan will be moving to LA from Atlanta to help us. I've also decided to renew my nursing license and go back to working in healthcare part-time.

Along with reconnecting with several significant people from my past, I also am blessed with good friends like Victoria, who has been with me for the birth of all my children and while I fought with DCFS over the years. She continues to be my support system. Out of everyone in my life, Victoria has been a constant, close friend for 21 years. I also am still very close to my best friend Steve Erhardt. He gave me the inspiration to follow my dreams and soar through life unscathed. We have a 30-year friendship. I love him dearly

I feel very lucky to have survived some of the scarier predicaments I found myself in, including very hard times with substance abuse. I'm blessed to have come out, given what I did. In some ways, my addiction is a big part of who I am today because it helped me turn myself around and stop being so self-destructive. Life is so much better clear-eyed.

Many women I met in the adult film industry were pimped out and drugged. Some were beaten and violently raped. Others were murdered. I'm lucky none of those things happened to me.

Of everything I've been through, the hardest to overcome was sexual abuse as a child. At a young age, children are so resilient that they stifle the hurt and learn to survive. It does impact you, however. In my case, I genuinely believe it led me to become an adult film star. Without that abuse, I don't think I would have been so open to exploiting my sexuality for financial gain. I believe my earlier abuse ingrained in me that sex was something you could use to get something in return.

At the same time, it's a person's choice whether they want to be a victim or not. I didn't want to be a victim. I was strong. I was not going to let my past define me.

As for what I would tell my daughter, should she come to me for advice about whether or not to become an adult film star, I would say no. We always want better for our daughters than what we've done, right?

I think back on all of the chances I took with my life. I think about all of the friends I have lost and feel very fortunate to have left the industry in good health. I thank God every day for my health, my beautiful children, and my sobriety.

I don't think I would have arrived at this place without going through pain and heartache. My best advice to someone who has big dreams is to put themselves in an achievable scenario, whether that be moving to LA, going to college, or leaving home.

My life was like an obstacle course. I didn't know what I wanted to be, so I just kept trying until I found it, guided by God's grace. All things considered, I'm at a good place in my life after a solid decade of struggling. I believe I'm here for a reason, which is why I wanted to share my story – the good times and the warts and scars – to hopefully inspire someone to follow their passions and dreams and not get sidetracked by mistakes and false turns.

I wouldn't change anything about my life because many of my accomplishments and the things that mean so much to me came to me through trial and error. I wasn't planning to have children, but my children are my life and I love them all more than anything in the world. The relationships with my children's fathers were built on my identity as Domonique Simone. That's who they met, not Deidre. I've come to peace with that fact.

Some people say that you have to hit rock bottom to realize the important things in life. That's definitely true in my case. All of my mistakes – from drugs to bad relationships – just made me start to learn myself and get the help that I needed. I wouldn't change a thing. I feel as if I came out on top, rising from the ashes.

It's funny how one's life seems to be in the stars. Decades ago, while on tour, I went to a gay bar in Boston with Steve. A guy walked up to me and suggested I go downstairs to get a psychic reading from his sister, who was the only other woman there that night. She told me I would have four children and that a friend would deceive me. She also said I was the reincarnation of Oshun, the river goddess in the Yoruba religion, who is associated with water, purity, fertility, love, and sensuality. She's considered one of the most powerful orishas, but she also possesses human attributes such as vanity, jealousy, and spite. There might be something to that.

Last night, I had a dream about my grandmother. Usually, when I dream of her, I can't see her face or reach her. This time, I woke up in my bedroom in my childhood home in the projects. I went downstairs looking for her then ran back upstairs because she wasn't in her bed. Sometimes in these dreams, I wake up and she is still there sleeping, but

I can count those times on only one hand.

In this dream, I was wearing a white sundress that flowed around my knees as I ran. It was a beautiful spring day and everything was sunny and green. For the first time, I wasn't a child in the dream. When I ran out the backdoor into the yard, I saw my grandmother walking away into the glimmery glow of a sunset. She was pulling the same wagon that she used to drag me around in.

I yelled, "Grandmommie, I was looking for you," and she turned around with a beautiful smile.

"Deirdre," she said. "I was just walking to the corner store."

I ran and hugged her, grabbing her hand as I turned to lead us home.

"Wait here," I said. "Let me just grab my shoes and I'll walk with you."

Up until now, I could never see her face or get close enough to touch her. This time I did. I finally found her. She's at peace and so am I.

My Grandmother

ACKNOWLEDGMENT

First and foremost, I would like to extend my deepest gratitude to God, who has guided me through the ebb and flow of life, granting me the strength to persevere and the gift of being able to share my story.

To my cherished children, you are the shining beacons in my life. Your existence has given me purpose and direction, and for that, I love you more than words can express.

My beloved Grandmother, Ethel, and my dear Uncle Jonathan, your unwavering support and guidance have been my pillars of strength. You have always been there to pull me back from the edge, inspiring me to live life to its fullest.

To my parents, who have loved me unconditionally through all of life's ups and downs, your unwavering love has been my rock.

A special thanks goes to the two Steves in my life. To Steve Erhardt, my makeup artist and a source of inspiration for this book, and to my other Steve, who stood by me through all the wild times and never ceased to believe in me.

Nyell, your motivation gave me the push I needed to weather the storm. And to Harvard Jones and Ann Marie Ballowe, your friendship has been a comforting blanket during trying times. Victoria, your unwavering loyalty through both good and bad times means the world to me.

I am immensely grateful to my photographers: Robert Ouano, Nick Saglimbeni, and Dave Bailey IV, who have used their lenses to beautifully encapsulate moments of my journey.

A heartfelt thanks to my team - Barbara Sanchez, my publicist, Sherry, my makeup artist (Beautybysherryo), Stacy Wesley, my hairstylist (Tangled Hair), and Andrea A Ward, my stylist. Your combined efforts have been invaluable. To Lilli Ortega from The Extreme Collections and my attorney, Gregory Daniels, thank you for your support.

To Jennifer Kocher, my writer, thank you for helping me navigate through the writing of this book. Your kindness and understanding have meant the world to me. And to Ellen Fike, your assistance in putting the final touches on the book was the icing on the cake.

The creative direction of this book would not have been possible without the expertise of Geoff Clark. A special mention to Switzon S. Wigfall, III "SSWIII", for the exquisite cover art and to Dave Bailey IV for the stunning cover photograph.

In this intricate ballet of life, we are all interconnected, our stories laced together to form a grand tapestry of human experience. Each individual I've thanked here has been an essential stitch in the fabric of my narrative, their impact forever engraved in my heart.

I've chosen to bare my soul in these pages, hoping that the transparency and raw truth of my story will resonate with others. To those who are walking through the valleys, know that peaks await. To those who are struggling, remember that the night is darkest before the dawn. My journey stands testament to the power of resilience, the promise of light at the end of the tunnel, and the potential for rebirth inherent in each of us.

This book is not just about my life, but a shared human experience. My trials and triumphs, my lows and highs, are mirrored in countless lives around the world. I hope my story serves as a beacon of hope and inspiration, a reminder that no matter how steep the mountain, it can be climbed.

To all who walk with me on this journey, thank you. You have not only helped me tell my story, you've become a part of it. And for that, I am eternally grateful. Here's to the strength within us, the bonds between us, and the stories yet to be told. Thank you for being a part of mine.

BREAKING BARRIERS AND BARING IT ALL

DOMONIQUE SIMONE

A STAR IS PORN

THE EXTRAORDINARY LIFE OF THE QUEEN OF ADULT ENTERTAINMENT

www.ingramcontent.com/pod-product-compliance
Ingram Content Group UK Ltd.
Pitfield, Milton Keynes, MK11 3LW, UK
UKHW062312290726
14090UKWH00018B/1025